LUCK
is *not* a plan for your
FUTURE

DESIGN YOUR TOMORROW TODAY

Leslie Gallery-Dilworth

BALBOA.
PRESS

A DIVISION OF HAY HOUSE

Balboa Press books may be ordered through booksellers or by contacting:

Balboa Press
A Division of Hay House
1663 Liberty Drive
Bloomington, IN 47403
www.balboapress.com
1 (877) 407-4847

Printed in the United States of America.

ISBN: 978-1-4525-1689-9 (sc)
ISBN: 978-1-4525-1691-2 (hc)
ISBN: 978-1-4525-1690-5 (e)

Library of Congress Control Number: 2014910755

Balboa Press rev. date: 07/10/2014

Luck? I don't know anything about luck. I've never banked on it and I'm afraid of people who do. Luck to me is something else: hard work— and realizing what is opportunity and what isn't.

—Lucille Ball

Am I Lucky?

I'm lucky to be able to live where I always dreamed of living, in the countryside near Santa Fe, New Mexico.

I'm lucky to have designed and built my dream house.

I'm lucky to live and work in far-off New Mexico when my office was in Washington, D.C.

I'm lucky to have enjoyed and respected all the people with whom I have worked.

I'm lucky to have a flexible work schedule while my sons were growing up, to take a month off in the summer and be there for my kids' vacations.

I'm lucky that I was able to dream up ideas and actually make them happen.

Eventually that comment "You are so lucky!" began to annoy me.

I know that I am very fortunate, but each time someone said to me, "You are so lucky," I thought, *Wait a second! It hasn't been luck*. It has happened by design, hard work, and the ability to recognize and take advantage of opportunities!

You *can* design your own luck!

Contents

Author's Note—Design Is a Framework 1

Design Is Imagining What *Can* Be 5

Four Steps, Four Commitments 7

You Can Have It All—Just Redefine "All" 13

Quite Literally Planting a Seed and Growing a Business 33

Stop Crying and Go for It 47

Opportunities Really Are Everywhere 59

When and How Is It Time for You to Move On 73

A Big Problem for Everyone Else Can Be an Even

    Bigger Opportunity for You 79

Rebuilding an Organization That Has Lost Its Way 93

A Few Detours 103

Coincidence Leads to Opportunity 111

Opportunity and Coincidence: Sleeping in my Dream House 113

Opportunity and Coincidence: Prince Charles, the

    Italian Garden, and Me 116

Opportunity and Coincidence: Two Wandering Englishmen 118

Opportunity and Coincidence: Rediscovering a

    Childhood Friend 120

Opportunity and Coincidence:

    The Wedding Gift to Each Other, Galisteo 122

Opportunity and Coincidence: An English Country Cottage 124

Opportunity and Coincidence: Looking over Her Shoulder 126

Opportunity and Coincidence:

    First Appearances Can Be Deceiving 127

Opportunity and Coincidence:

    When My Father Met My Professor 130

Conclusion 137

Author's Note
Design Is a Framework

You can pick up this book for fifteen minutes or read it all in one sitting.

(Secret: I often start with last chapters!)

These stories may be amusing, but each has important lessons. The stories begin with pursuing opportunities; they conclude with the lessons I learned and a final question for you. Each story may spark new insights for you in turning your ideas into realities.

I believe that coincidences can definitely lead to opportunities, provided you are receptive to coincidence and recognize how that coincidence can lead to an opportunity. There is a section at the end of the book on opportunities born from coincidences.

Can you really design *all* aspects of your life, all the time? Of course not.

And neither would anyone want to. I love being open to new opportunities and meeting new people. The better you understand your talents, and the more you know about what you want, what your priorities and values are, the closer you will come to achieving both your short-term and long-term goals.

I have taken a nontraditional path in my life. I have zigzagged my way to success ... success by *my* definition.

In sixth grade, or around the time that Frank Lloyd Wright proposed a mile-high tower for Chicago, I decided I wanted to be an architect and design cities, skyscrapers, and houses. My little brother's sandbox became the setting for my miniature cities and parks.

I now am a licensed architect, but I have never been an architect in the traditional sense, nor have I ever built a single building (except for my own home). In 1990, one of the Philadelphia newspapers called me "an influential architect who has never built a single building"!

What I *have* built are successful organizations. I have designed and implemented significant projects, founded financially successful publications, created and produced large public events, and resurrected a failing national organization. I have influenced places and the way people think about their environment. That has been my goal, always. That has been my contribution.

My journey may appear to wander, but the framework has always been the same. Rather than take the most direct expressway or the turnpike routes, I have taken scenic detours and picturesque side roads. Being open to these detours has made for a rich and varied life. Even as an architect I have not made the traditional choices. By coming from another direction with the discipline of architecture, I have influenced the design and quality of our surroundings. I have certainly observed that the most direct route is not necessarily the best path to your destination. It may not even take you where you can be most effective. Within the framework of my overall design, the zigzags have transported me to places I had not imagined.

Without too much anxiety (but definitely some), I have integrated my family life and my business life with satisfaction, living where I wanted, working the schedules that I chose to with people I have admired, on projects that were invigorating for me and useful for my community.

I have not designed my life or my career from start to finish. But I have been open to opportunities within the framework of architecture and design. Having a framework in which to make those choices enabled me to build a career and a life based on possibilities, not limitations.

- What is your goal?
- What will be your contribution?
- What are your possibilities?

Design is a plan for arranging elements in such a way as best to accomplish a particular purpose.

—Charles Eames

Design Is Imagining What *Can* Be

Some of the best designs allow for flexibility within an overall framework.

For a professional architect or designer, the process of designing is an adventure. The blank surface can be both intimidating and freeing.

Design as a process is open and joyful. In the design process, information is gathered and organized. Ideas are challenged. Alternatives are explored.

Design is imagining what can be. In the very process of imagining what can be, you will explore and reveal many paths and alternatives—evaluate, adjust, modify, and often reject. This is different from the scientific process, where you start from the position of what is known and build out from there.

Design is a process that *always* leads to a solution.

Eric Karjaluoto of smashLAB, a creative agency, says, "Design is a disciplined pursuit aimed at producing sensible, functional work for clients." I certainly agree.

In this case you are your own client. *You* are the designer of *your life*, and you don't need a degree in design to accomplish this.

As you design your core concept and your vision, your goal will become more clear to you. When this happens you will continue to test your opportunities and decisions against this vision, until your vision, your decisions, your opportunities, and your challenges meet.

Four Steps, Four Commitments

Using the word *design* is a habit for me and a prejudice. We are all designers. Each of us is the designer of our own life. As an architect and a landscape architect, I regard almost every problem or situation as a design opportunity. In our lives there are many opportunities to incorporate the design process.

Here are four steps and four commitments that will provide an effective road map toward achieving your goals.

Four Basic Steps

1. Identify the problem or opportunity.
2. Determine the "ideal."
3. Describe the "mess" (the current situation).
4. Create a specific road map with the specific steps required to move from the "mess" to the "ideal."

You can make your idea real; you can make it all happen. You can have a positive impact on yourself, your family, and your community.

To make that happen, four key commitments are required.

Four Commitments

1. Explore your imagination and vision, without saying "It's impossible."
2. Be consistent in persistence and determination.
3. Seek out collaborators.
4. Take action. Move forward. Move through your fears.

These maxims apply equally to designing for yourself as an individual and for your family. You can also design your vision for your business or organization and even design for a specific project within your business or organization. This process also works for accomplishing goals for improving your community.

Your Four Basic Steps Worksheet

1. Identify the problem or opportunity.

2. What is your "ideal"?

3. Describe your "mess" (the current situation).

4. Create a specific road map with the specific steps required to move from the "mess" to the "ideal." Exactly what has to be done, how and when, and then what will it cost?
   (You will need more than this amount of space)

Your Four Commitments Worksheet

1. Explore your imagination and vision! Nothing is impossible!

2. I am determined to ...

3. My best collaborators are ...

4. I am taking action, moving forward, moving through my fears by ...

Perhaps the most costly disassembly in which our culture has been engaged, is the disaggregation of life itself into work, play, learning, and inspiration.

—Russell L. Ackoff, *Re-Creating the Corporation: A Design of Organizations for the 21st Century*

You Can Have It All—
Just Redefine "All"

In this chapter, you will discover

- that "all" is a moving target;
- how to implement "integration" rather than "balance"; and
- that your choices are your framework.

Rethink what "all" means!

No one ever tells you how hard it is going to be to excel in your career, nurture your family, and maintain yourself and your relationships. Most people are not entirely truthful about the energy required or the stress you will most likely feel, striving to have it all or attempting to find the perfect balance. You watch films and TV shows and read stories about women who juggle everything with ease. Families look so happy. That was going to be me!

As a teenager I used to imagine being an architect, stirring food on the stove with one hand and having a set of drawings in the other, while smiling lovingly at my family. Yes, smiling, with peace and quiet all around me, quiet children playing nicely on the floor. I *knew* I could do it all. The thought that it might be difficult never entered my mind. And absolutely no one ever broached the subject with me—not in high school, not in college, not in graduate school, and certainly not out in the professional world! Just how difficult juggling all this is seemed to be a well-kept secret among women professionals until recently. This news is now everywhere.

In my early twenties, I knew only one female architect who had children, and she was my professor. The very few other female architects I knew were either unmarried, married with no children, or married to an architect and not working.

Young women and men as well asked so many times "How do you balance family and career?" Before I had children I never asked myself that question. The answer is that I did *not* balance my family, my career, and me! I don't think that is possible or realistic. What I did do was *integrate* my family, my career, and me. "Balance" to me means that everything is very tidy and always in order. I am not sure I have, or that anyone has, completely balanced *their* work and home lives.

Your day, *your* week, *your* month, even your year is not the balanced class schedule you had in high school—forty-five-minute periods, then move on to the next. If that is what you are looking for, you're setting yourself up for frustration and disappointment. I would be skeptical of anyone who claims they have "balanced" their work and their family. Ask them just what that means.

Balance to me comes with the feeling or knowledge that you're not doing anything well enough, and that everyone is probably a little dissatisfied with you. And you are probably dissatisfied with you as well. Why? Because you are probably still thinking that you should be able to do it all and achieve balance. And do all this with ease.

So, balance? I don't think so.

Let's achieve integration. We *can* do that.

A colleague and friend who just turned fifty has two children, a supportive husband, and a successful international design practice. When we discussed her balancing act, she suggested the word *integration* might be more accurate. Absolutely! *Integration* is the right word and far more doable. Integration is a more realistic and, I think, healthier goal.

You can't just totally separate your life into chunks.

What is the difference between a job and a passion? I think of a job as something you leave emotionally at the end of the workday— whereas you probably think about a passion and achieving a vision much more of the time. This thinking is not limited to any specific time frame.

Integration takes into account the ebb and flow of your family, your life partner, your needs, and your work. Sometimes family demands the most attention and energy. At other times it is work, and occasionally it may even be you who needs the attention.

You have to be extremely flexible; you have to be able to switch gears quickly. That is why women are good executives. Consider the skills, organization, and flexibility required to raise children and run a household.

Remember: "All" is a moving target! Let's look at some major choices that will bring you closer to your integration of family and career.

Choice: A Life Partner

Another essential for career and personal success is your choice of a life partner. Many people say this is number one. Your partner or spouse must share responsibilities and childcare 50-50 (sometimes more), and hopefully stops counting the times shared. This person really wants you to be successful. Not just in theory or in abstract conversations, but in reality, every day.

I had an employee once, a fantastic person. She was beautiful, smart, kind, and extremely competent. She was married to a young doctor, a resident in psychiatry. She wanted very much to be an architect, and he often said he wanted her to be an architect.

What he really wanted was to be able to *say* that his wife was an architect! During the years I knew him, it became clear he did not want to support her through the process of becoming an architect. He clearly would not support her in being an architect, either.

A friend was pursuing a journalism career, but her husband kept accepting better jobs in different cities. Each time they moved she had to start all over in an entry-level job. At first she didn't object, because she enjoyed the warm, sunny places they lived, but her career was going nowhere, and he was growing more and more distant. The fourth time he decided to relocate, this time to a city in a cold climate, without even consulting her. Now she knew for certain, their marriage was on the rocks.

Selecting your life partner is a huge decision; it is about more than just being in love.

Choice: Having Children

If you demand peace and quiet, order and neatness, then do not have children. For me nothing was so hard as being home all the time with little children, even though they are the loves of my life. Some people are good at that and enjoy it. I admire such people. I had some good friends like that.

Even one child changes your life, and with more than one, well ... sometimes I felt like giving up my professional ambitions. The conflicts and pulls on me were exhausting. And the demands I put on myself could be oppressive and unnecessary. You may have a different opinion; I am just telling you my view.

Maybe you know someone who just appears to be gliding through all that.

I am not that someone. And it's probably not you either. That is okay.

There is joy, though! I loved watching my children grow from babies into toddlers, into little people, into teenagers, and now adults. The entire process is amazing, tiring, and somewhat perplexing. But I would never, ever trade having children and raising them.

I love babies. I loved nursing. I even made all my own baby food. My first child was relatively easy, and I thought that was because I was such a competent mother. Maybe. But then my second child, who was so cute, was just the opposite in behavior as a baby. My conclusion is that within a limited parameter babies are born the way they are and how they are going to be.

I had tried working from home. One afternoon I received a phone call from an architectural supplier who did not know me. While we were on the phone, the dog ran into my son's play table and scattered blocks all over the floor. My three-year-old son was screaming, and the puppy was barking, and of course that woke the baby, who added his own cries to the cacophony. With all this commotion in the background, the supplier said to me, "Are you sure you're an architect?"

Crying babies and crashing castles of blocks may be a cute scene in a movie, but this doesn't work in the real business world. It is just not professional. Our society is not quite ready for this scenario. And this environment is not conducive to doing your best work *or* your best parenting. It is hard to concentrate and focus your attention.

What definitely doesn't work is merging taking-care-of-kid time with taking-care-of-work time. Both will be short-changed, in my observation and opinion. I adored my babies and then my toddlers. But I didn't like being at home all the time.

Staying home all the time was not very rewarding to me. In fact, it was discouraging. I am a not a great housekeeper. Every day I was surrounded with reminders of failure and frustration: always more dishes to wash, laundry to do, toys to pick up. I viewed these circumstances as evidence of incompetence. Everywhere I looked, I saw failure: failure to have the laundry done and folded, failure to have all the dishes washed and put away, failure to have the toys picked up. Nothing ever was really finished. There was always another toy, another glass, another article of clothing to be washed.

For many summers we shared a house at the beach with other families. One of our housemates was very organized, with lots of schedules and lots of charts telling everyone what they were to do that day. She liked to say to me, with superiority, "I don't know how you have a job with such responsibility. You are so unorganized, so casual about housework." (In my defense, it was summer—and my vacation.)

I mentioned this to the head of a big foundation in the context of my being somewhat disorganized and having lots of balls in the air. He responded by saying, "I know her. She may be very organized, but what has she accomplished? You may appear disorganized, but you know how to get things done and how to make ideas happen."

Don't confuse efficiency and organization with effectiveness.

New-mother happiness brings challenges and joy
Leslie and Wyatt, 1975

Choice: Time with Children

Being home for my children, picking them up at day care, and being with them on vacation were my priorities. Whenever there was a choice, the kids were the priority. That was my point of reference.

Throughout the year I could guarantee there would be times when everyone was dissatisfied with me (sometimes individually, and sometimes all at the same time). My office wanted me there more, my kids wanted me at their games, my husband wanted to go away on a long weekend, and I just wanted to go to the hairdresser and read a fashion magazine!

Yes, you are normal; this is stressful. You can handle it.

Not being able to completely satisfy everyone is just a reality to which I had to become accustomed. Accepting this reality reduces much of the stress.

Choice: Where You Live

We lived in a beautiful location. We had a couple acres on the city border, fronting on an arboretum. The English Cotswold stone house looked over rolling hills and an apple orchard. It was hard to believe we were within the city boundaries. I loved the house and enjoyed the setting. I fell in love with this place the minute I saw it. Yet I was so unhappy while living there.

The downside to our little enclave was that there were no sidewalks, no immediate neighbors, and no convenient public transportation. And no women in the neighborhood worked outside the home.

I could not go anywhere without getting in the car and driving. Even to go for a walk with the stroller on a sidewalk, I had to drive. There were no day-care facilities in the entire area.

All of these considerations together made for a big mistake in location! With children what you want and need are immediate neighbors, preferably with children your children's ages. You want sidewalks for strolling with the baby. You want company. You want a bus stop or train stop nearby, within walking distance. You want day-care facilities in the neighborhood.

Neither my then-husband, John, nor I had ever lived in the suburbs; we were city people. We had never had two small children. We did not realize what really matters in choosing a home and a neighborhood.

Choose your neighborhood to make life easy. And ask all the questions before falling in love with a place.

Choice: Where You Work

As soon as I made the decision to go back to work outside my home, I began considering my ideal, my current situation, and my doable ideal. Here were my options:

1. I could work in a large firm where they were doing big buildings, and I would learn a lot about how to put buildings and complex projects together (remember my dreams of skyscrapers).

The downside of this option was that in a profession known for long hours and very few women, I would not be able to say, "I have to leave to pick up my kids" or "I can't work this weekend."

That would not have been tolerated. At that time there were very few women in architecture, and their challenges in balancing work and home life were simply not considered a priority or even acceptable. My team members would have thought I was not carrying my weight. I would have felt guilty, they would have been angry, and the atmosphere would have become unpleasant.

So that was out. It would be the wrong kind of stress.

2. I could work on my own, but I would also be responsible for all the marketing, design, construction supervision, and administration, until I could build up a real practice with sufficient clients to finance a staff.

And of course, at the same time, be there for my children.

3. I could work in a small firm with a more relaxed environment, but where there was little room for advancement or ability to work on interesting projects.

4. I could do something else, like teaching (again).

Leslie Gallery-Dilworth

Then an opportunity came along that was a very good "Something Else." Just at this time I met with the executive director at the Philadelphia chapter of the American Institute of Architects (AIA), who was moving on to another job and looking for a replacement. Here I would answer to a board of directors but basically be my own boss. I could work on many different kinds of projects that would influence architecture and the environment.

I could have more regular hours, without the peer pressure of an architect's office. This environment would be a better kind of stress.

As an assistant professor of architecture at the University of Texas, taking Wyatt to the office, 1976

Choice: Who Does the Laundry?

This is not a frivolous question. The answer has many repercussions for your career and family. This is important.

When my boys were seven and nine, I had just one inflexible rule in the house: I had to be able to see the floor of their room once a week. (That coincided with the day that the cleaning service came.)

On one of these days, I happened to open their laundry hamper. It was filled with neatly folded clean clothes—clothes that had neither been worn nor put away. The clothes had been on the floor. Throwing them in the hamper was my sons' efficient way to get everything off the floor and make their room look clean.

Upon seeing this, I thought, "No way am I going to be washing and folding their clothes and have them throw them back in the wash." How clever the boys thought they were.

So I introduced them both to the washing machine and dryer. I told them I was never, ever again going to do their wash. I showed them how to sort their clothes, which settings to use, and how to fold the clothes from the dryer.

I explained that I really didn't care if they wore dirty clothes to school. If they wanted clean clothes, they would have to wash them themselves. Of course, they thought this was a momentary outburst of anger and that I would get over it. But I didn't. I stuck to it. I never wavered, not even to this day. (They are now in their thirties.) Eventually they got the idea and washed their clothes when they wanted clean apparel.

Was this cruel? I do not think so. I was working, and I was recently divorced and a single mom. I was busy too. At the time they thought I was a mean mommy, until they became used to this routine.

When they went to college, they each called to boast about how proud they were of themselves. They were the only guys in their dorm who knew how to do their own laundry. They have also ironed their own clothes, always. I am a terrible ironer. When I finish ironing something, it looks like I need to start again. So I never bought anything that needed ironing, for me or for my sons.

When one of them wanted something that needed to be ironed, I explained that I did not iron clothes for myself, so I certainly wasn't going to buy something for them that had to be ironed, unless they would iron it. (Eventually my father showed them how to iron shirts and pants.)

One time, when he was in his early twenties, one of my sons was home from college and was late for a date. Very apologetically he said, "Mom, I know you will not do our ironing, and I have never asked you to, but I am so late, and these are linen slacks. Could you possibly, just this once, iron these for me while I take a shower?" I gave in. This was an exception. *I'm not heartless, after all.*

After ironing the slacks carefully, I was about to hand them to him. He took one look at them and said, "You really can't iron, can you?" He took them from me and ironed them quickly himself. And they looked much better.

It's about More than Washing Clothes

I have met women who complain about how busy they are; they don't have time for their work because they are doing everything at home. Their kids are teenagers. I ask who is doing their laundry. Not the kids or the partner, that's for sure. When I suggest that others could do the laundry and that it would actually be good for all of them, the response is, "Oh, never" or "It would use too much water." Or that it is too much trouble to show them.

This is not really about washing clothes. It's about much more. So stop bitching. This is a household. You are doing your part. Everyone else needs to do their part as well. It will give them self-respect and independence.

- Everyone talks about balance.
- They need to be thinking "integration."
- What does integration mean for you?

Lessons Learned about "Balance"

- Achieving balance in career and family doesn't work. Integrating career and family is realistic.
- Having children and a career is hard work. It requires energy, perseverance, flexibility, and patience. It's hard raising kids. Not everyone should have kids.
- Invest in good staff at home and at the office.
- Your life partner is critical to your success as a parent and in your career.
- Live in a convenient place ... a mom-and-kid-friendly place.
- Listen to your frustration and anxieties. Do something positive to move beyond them. Look after your mental and physical health.
- Delegate at home and at the office.
- Choose your stress!
- Remember—being highly organized doesn't always mean being highly effective!

Combining business and family:
Leslie takes Wyatt and Andrew to meet
architect Charles Moore, 1988

The very substance of the ambitious is merely the shadow of a dream.

—William Shakespeare

Quite Literally Planting a Seed
and Growing a Business

Getting laid off may not be the end of the world! Don't be a victim! Create your own opportunity!

In this chapter, you'll discover how to

- recognize an opportunity/need;
- start a business with severe money and time constraints;
- find a vision of your business;
- design a brand and style for the business; and
- learn on the job, which is okay!

After graduate school I was working for an architecture and urban design firm. I had been there only a couple of months when they downsized. As the most recently hired, I was the first to be let go.

One of the firm's partners was building a large townhouse and garden. Knowing my background was in landscape architecture, he asked me to design his garden. Now, this wasn't just any little old garden. It was three townhouses wide, in the center of the Philadelphia. The garden was very large, as was the budget I was given. Because of the scale of the space, my design was primarily architectural, with some plants, trees, and shrubs.

As the trucks laden with flowers and shrubs drove through the narrow old streets of the historic Philadelphia neighborhood, I noticed passers-by were following them. I felt like the Pied Piper or the purveyor of popsicles. When the trucks pulled into the parking area behind the house, people wanted to buy the plants off the trucks. I explained to everyone that these plants were for a specific house.

I realized that these city folk had no place nearby to purchase plants or other supplies for their city gardens, rooftops, and balconies. Nothing at the suburban garden centers was the right scale for urban spaces. The planting and growing conditions in the city were different from those in the suburbs. But these Center City Philadelphia residents were forced to drive at least thirty or forty-five minutes to shop at one of the suburban garden centers. I filed this in the back of my mind, thinking this might be an opportunity for someone other than me, as I had never had a real garden.

At the same time, I was involved in renovating a large warehouse in what is now called Old City in Philadelphia. It was then an area of active, as well as historic deserted, warehouses, each with beautiful architectural character. In the middle of these historic warehouses, a few urban pioneers (including me) lived on a block called Elfreth's Alley, which had been preserved from colonial times. As I walked the narrow old streets of this unique neighborhood, it seemed that another beautiful old building was being torn down.

I convinced my boyfriend that we had a duty as architects to do something about the destruction and loss of these wonderful old buildings. We had to set an example of what could be done. These buildings could be transformed. We had to show by example that these renovated mixed-use historic buildings could thrive.

We could not wait for someone else. We had to make the decision, take the chance, and act *now*. It was up to us!!

The Positive Results of a Negative Response!

We found a wonderful warehouse with cast iron facades to renovate: a large, four-story building on a corner, with double-height floors and beautiful floor-to-ceiling windows on three sides. We intended to live on the top floor, have another rental loft on the third floor, and rent offices on the second floor. It was to be a mixed-use building with retail shops on the ground floor.

We went to the banks for financing. No bank would give us a loan. Every banker said, "No. Absolutely not! Who would ever want to live in a loft in a warehouse, in a neighborhood of warehouses?"

Well, *we* wanted to. (By the way, thirty-five years later, all the warehouses have been renovated, and the lofts and apartments are some of the hottest places to live in Philadelphia. So much for bankers and their insight and lack of imagination!)

In the end my friend John, who later became my husband, financed the renovation with his savings. We did most of the work ourselves and subcontracted the mechanical, the electrical, and the plumbing.

There was no roof, and pigeons lived on the top floor.

Clearly, we required a certain fearlessness or naïveté.

It was late June when we started. While we renovated the upper floors, we needed to generate income quickly, to cover the monthly payments for the building. I had remembered my previous experience designing my boss's townhouse garden. I suggested, "Center City needs an urban garden center. We could open one on the ground floor! There is no competition in the area! But it would have to open before the fall planting season." That meant before Labor Day, less than two months away.

The Positive Results of Naïveté, Energy, and Enthusiasm!

Our need for immediate rental income meant I did not have time to fret about my inexperience or dwell on what I did not know. We set to work renovating a small portion of the ground floor facing the street. Having no money and very limited time, we did the absolute minimum. We cleaned up the front forty-foot-square area of the ground floor; painted the walls, ceiling, and floor; and installed new, inexpensive, standard fluorescent lighting tubes in a geometric pattern.

City Gardens, exterior, 1972

We designed and distributed eye-catching notices announcing "CITY GARDENS OPENING." These were hand-delivered to hundreds of residents in the nearest neighborhoods. We also had a big, handsome sign painted, "CITY GARDENS, Inc."

City Gardens proved to be an excellent opportunity for us and a highly appreciated resource for the city dwellers. As a new business owner without financing, I was working seven days a week in the store all day and bookkeeping at home in the evenings. Everything was new to me, and I was learning so much that I had not learned in school or at architecture firms. While I had not paid attention to my courses on plant materials while in graduate school, I was now studying those very same books and class notes every evening. Botanical names, so foreign to me while a student, were now just rolling off my tongue!

Soon I had built a staff and had a payroll to meet and garden construction projects to oversee. This led to architectural projects as well for my landscape clients.

Shaping the Business Vision

I envisioned City Gardens as an oasis in the city. City Gardens had a strong point of view, and a strong brand. It was not just a plant store. The store needed to offer everything the city gardener could want, from supplies to books to furniture to houseplants, annuals, shrubs, and full-grown trees. With a total of only $2,500 as seed money, we had to be especially resourceful. Even in 1970 this was not a lot of money. I negotiated an arrangement with a suburban nursery to carry their large trees and shrubs on consignment in exchange for my using their nursery to install all the landscaping and gardens. Unlike the trees and shrubs, the houseplants were purchased outright at the greenhouses. City Gardens had not yet established a credit history. Each Monday, the day the store was closed, I made the trip to the greenhouses to personally select each tropical plant, rather than just calling the nursery and having them delivered. Why go to this trouble? Every houseplant had to be perfect; we could not afford an unsold plant. Plants were inventory, which translated to money. Suddenly, since the plants meant dollars, I began to develop a "green thumb."

City Gardens, interior, with wooden pallets
used as display cases.

Marimekko fabric became staff smocks, adding color and
design to our branding effort. The same fabrics were also
used as space dividers hanging from the ceiling.

Designing the Brand and Style

The decor of the store had to be striking and unique but simple, cheap, and effective. While we were imaginative designers, we had very limited financial resources. Across the street was a wholesale awning/canvas supplier.

We bought large strips of bright orange awning to hang from the ceiling on pipes across the back wall, which concealed the fact that the majority of space behind the curtain was unfinished, and at the same time the canvas created a colorful, striking image for the passersby.

To create inexpensive display stands and shelving, we used unfinished lumber as the shelving with exposed brackets. Some well-designed pieces of modern wicker furniture created a sitting area under the full-sized trees on display from the nursery. Discarded wooden packing crates—which we collected from the sidewalks and warehouses around the neighborhood—were the perfect size and price (free!) on which to display houseplants and create defined smaller areas within the overall space.

One day a *Philadelphia Magazine* reporter who wrote about design and hot trends stopped by. She loved the look of the store and wrote a glowing article about how "natural" was the next big thing. (For us it was the only thing, because it was also the least expensive thing.) Many customers came as a result of that article. The store enjoyed a real buzz.

Over the next eighteen months, we increased the size of the store several times, extending the original 40 x 40 area until we filled the entire first floor of 4,000 square feet. We transformed a section of the store into a highly visible design studio that brought in design commissions and home renovations as well. Soon City Gardens became *the* place to gather on weekends. We began to serve coffee and tea. We wanted people to linger and think of City Gardens as a destination.

I envisioned this store not so much as a store, but as an interior garden in the center of the city. City Gardens was a place where people could come to buy a book, a vase, a tool, soil, or a very big tree. It was full service. You could get advice on any question regarding plants and planting. We loved our customers (with a couple of exceptions), and they seemed to love us back.

And now I was designing not just gardens, but residential renovations—my first love! This became my first step in designing houses on my own. Now I was working with attorneys on contracts, and with contractors, and learning to manage staff.

Reinforcing our vision of a public garden within the city, we reached out to local schools and community organizations. On weekday mornings the public schools used some of the space for environmental classes. On Sunday mornings the Pennsylvania Horticultural Society held workshops with their experts, for their members, in our store.

By then we had an excellent staff, and we even had simple but eye-popping uniforms and a bright orange mini-pickup truck! City Gardens, the urban garden center, had consistency in its branding details and great style! All of it initially financed by $2,500—and of course our creativity and hard work.

From this first basic step—identifying a problem as an opportunity—I learned how to direct a staff and work directly with clients, vendors, and contractors. I also was exposed to construction documentation and supervision, as well as design opportunities. I would not have been exposed to these challenges in such a short amount of time were I still employed in someone else's architecture office.

After three years of this, another opportunity presented itself, quite unexpectedly. My husband and I were both invited to teach in the School of Architecture and Planning at the University of Texas in Austin.

With mixed emotions we decided to leave our spacious loft apartment.

And although I had wonderful, honest staff who all worked hard and were excellent managers when I was there, when I returned for a visit the store was looking shabby. Sales were down and clients were disappearing. A small business does not have a lot of room for poor decisions or poor service. You also have to be on top of the finances and balance sheet every day.

This was a learning experience for me: some employees do best when the owner is around. Without me, the staff just didn't notice the finer details of what made the place sparkle. Some people are managers and good at implementing ideas, but that does not make them entrepreneurs. And my interest was elsewhere; I was no longer paying close enough attention. I was focusing on teaching and also expecting our first baby.

After a year I had to decide to sell or close the business, so we sold City Gardens. It was not an easy time. We sold it at a loss, but at least the rental income would be assured for the future. I learned a lot from this experience: how to start a business, manage a business, and sell a business.

- What seeds are you planting?

Lessons Learned from City Gardens

- Have an eye and ear for opportunity.
- Having insufficient funds does not have to be a total limitation.
- Have a clear point of view, and a strong brand to differentiate yourself.
- Create a consistent identity with mailings, cards, and signs, and extend that "look" to the interior, the exterior, the uniforms, and the vehicles.
- Provide outstanding customer service.
- Absentee ownership does not always pay. A good manager is not always a good leader.
- Have a good attorney and accountant, and pay close attention regularly to the finances.
- Don't forget to pay yourself. You are a business expense.
- When you make a decision, don't look back. Just work hard to make it work.
- As to the warehouse renovation, it doesn't always pay financially to be the first in the neighborhood. Don't invest a lot of money in a building you do not own (we had a long-term lease and first option for purchase).
- *And*, most of all, be prepared to work hard, and then even harder than you expected.

Life begins at the end of your comfort zone.

—Neale Donald Walsch

Stop Crying and Go for It

In this chapter, you'll discover how to

- admit and come to terms with being unhappy and unfulfilled;
- prepare for an interview (with a selection committee or an entire board);
- discuss salary needs and expectations;
- know and establish your own priorities;
- know when it makes sense to go to work even if you just break even financially; and
- answer questions tactfully that legally you should not be asked.

Returning to Philadelphia from four years in Austin, Texas, my first husband, John, and I bought a rambling stone home with an orchard in the suburbs. We decided not return to our loft downtown because of the long staircase of double-height floors, without an elevator. I had visions of slipping on the steps with the baby, both of us being seriously injured. So for the first time in our lives, we became suburbanites ... totally reliant on a car for even the simplest of things, such as a walk in the park. I felt so isolated!

One gray and icy winter day, I was running errands, eight months pregnant and holding the hand of my two-year-old, when I ran into a former classmate from architecture school. He already had his own successful firm. We shared pleasant greetings, and then he looked directly at me and said, "What are you doing these days?"

I thought, "Are you blind? What do you think I'm I doing?" But calmly and matter-of-factly (and even with a smile), I said, "Well, I have a two-year-old and am eight months pregnant."

He responded by saying, "Yes, I see that, but what are you *really* doing?"

For over thirty years, that incident has stayed with me. Why? Because what he said to me was what I already had been thinking to myself. I realize this now, of course.

On the other hand, is this an example of his limited thinking as well? He knew me as an architect—nothing else. That is what he expected from me, not the mommy and pregnant person. And perhaps he discounted the stuff that mommies do! His wife had always had sole responsibility for taking care of him and their children. (No wonder his firm was thriving.)

Half a year later, when my second child was about six months old, I realized that I had to get back to my profession. I wanted to become a good architect. I was losing valuable time.

I was also losing my sense of humor. I thought I was losing my identity. I was not even appreciating what was good about my life. I had so much, yet I was so dissatisfied.

I stopped by the Philadelphia chapter of the American Institute of Architects, to browse in their bookstore. The executive director saw me and mentioned that he was resigning to be the dean at Drexel University's architecture school. He told me that the AIA would be looking for a new executive director. "You should apply; you would be perfect," he said.

Did I agree? Well, kind of. Later in the day, while driving home from downtown, I told my husband about the encounter. He thought the position was perfect for me and that I would be perfect for them. My sensible response? I started crying, saying they would never hire me, so why bother going after the job? He replied, "If you don't go after that job, you have no right ever to complain about being at home or not developing your career."

He made sense. I decided to face my fears of rejection, put my ego aside, and go all out for this opportunity—that is, after I cried my eyes out thinking I would never ever get hired. This position would be perfect, I wouldn't have to work weekends or evenings, and I wouldn't have the peer pressure of an architectural firm. I would have a staff. I could initiate interesting projects. I could be the boss, answerable to a board of directors. It would be challenging and fun.

And besides, this would just be for a few years, because I was going to be an architect designing and building award-winning buildings.

By that time I was the mother of two boys, aged nine months and three years. I had been at home for eighteen months, which seemed so long. I wanted to return to my profession and the land of adult interaction.

Rather than being intimidated by the concept of meeting with a selection committee of six men in a smoky room, drinking bourbon, I thought the interview process would be fun. I was delighted to have a reason to change out of my blue jeans with peanut butter on the knees, and the shirt with spit-up on the shoulder. Wearing a costume of grown-up clothes, I looked forward to talking to real adults who were professionals in my field.

I had made the short list. Now I would meet with the entire board.

The formal interview process was challenging. I worked so hard to prepare for the interviews. Asking myself all the questions that an intelligent board should ask, I practiced and rehearsed my responses. I even called a good friend, renowned female architect (one of the few at that time) Denise Scott Brown and asked her how she would respond to questions about being a woman and a mother. These questions, of course, would be illegal because of recently passed affirmative action legislation, but I knew I would be asked anyway. If I refused to answer, the board would hold that against me; they would think I was argumentative and an obstructionist. They might even think I was—*gasp*—a feminist! So when the board actually asked me those types of questions, I was prepared.

Responding sweetly, I said, "You are probably unaware that you are legally not allowed to ask me questions regarding the care of my children or how I will be able to be a responsible mother or what kind of arrangements I will make to travel. But I am happy to answer your other questions and respond to any valid concerns."

I continued by saying, "Most of you are parents, and you manage, as I will, too." Of course, most had a wife at home but that was the end of the discussion. I never directly answered their inappropriate questions.

Then there were two more interviews with the entire board of directors of twelve to twenty men and one woman. (Alert: if you are a woman, another woman is not automatically on your side. Some women can be territorial, especially with other women. This particular woman had never married and had no children, and she was neither sympathetic nor supportive.)

To determine the critical issues and what would make for a good director, I had interviewed past presidents and people active within the organization. They had never hired a woman before, but I had an advantage because I was now an architect—a fully registered architect. (Credentials absolutely do count.)

After all these interviews I was finally hired. Later, I learned that their primary reservations had been that I was too opinionated, I had children, and my husband held an important position within the city. (What if I disagreed with a city position? They had heard I was bossy. I am.)

I also learned an important lesson about salary. They asked me what salary I wanted before they made me an offer. Thinking I was very clever, I said, "Whatever you are paying the current director will be acceptable to me." The current director was a man, and I said that because I did not want them to pay me less than they were paying a man, which was common practice at the time. When they told me his salary, I was shocked; it was so much lower than I expected. But of course I couldn't say anything, because I had now boxed myself in.

Leslie Gallery-Dilworth

Was Ninety Dollars a Week Worth This?

Between child care and business expenses, I was not really going to make any money. At the most, I figured I might break even. Was taking this job worth it? *Absolutely.* It was an investment in my future. And this position would lead to many opportunities. I also regained my self-worth, which made me much nicer to be around at home.

As director of the Foundation for Architecture, I often met with various boards and city agencies. Selection committee for the Philadelphia Orchestra meets to choose their new architect. This "men's club" meeting was typical of the times.

The Men's Club

On my first day of my new job at the AIA, the CEO of a large international architecture and engineering firm invited me to lunch at what had once been a men's luncheon club. Wearing my architect's costume—new blue blazer, new khaki skirt, silk blouse—I was looking forward to our appointment. The room was very elegant and very quiet … a nice change from home with two kids.

A waiter came to take our order. Instead of thinking about architecture, I thought, *They are actually going to bring my food to me! I am sitting at a real grown-up table, with breakable china dishes and glass glasses.*

My host leaned over and said, in all seriousness, "How does it feel too be back at work?"

I thought (but did not say), *Back at work? Are you kidding? This is a vacation! I'm not eating peanut butter and jelly at my kids' little oak table. I'm wearing real clothes, not my denim wraparound skirt, and there will be no banana handprints on my knees when I get up. And it is so quiet here. I am talking to a grown-up. I am not being interrupted. This is a vacation.*

What I did enthusiastically say was, "Great! Looking forward to the challenges!"

Looking around the room, I noticed there were no other women. The tables were full of men in suits talking in hushed voices. And I thought, *He has no idea how hard it is being a full-time mother and how isolated one gets to feeling.*

So … if this is working, then so far, I like being at "work."

Determining Your Boundaries, Establishing Your Priorities

What about my children?

Being home for my children, picking them up at day care, and taking them on vacation were important considerations to me. My top priority was my relationship with my children. Whenever there was a choice or a conflict, the children came first. My husband and I shared this commitment.

I was very clear about that to myself, my staff, and my board of directors.

Be clear, firm, and reassuring, not argumentative or apologetic. This is not always easy or without tension. None of this is easy. No one ever told me that, so I am telling you that.

After a year, I introduced the subject of taking off a full month in the summer. The board was quite apprehensive about the well-being of the organization. I explained that if our staff could not function well for a month without me, that would mean I was not a very good manager. Their fears were reasonable. I acknowledged their concerns and assured them I would be available if I were needed. At the end of the month, everything had gone smoothly, and from then on the summer schedule became a non-issue.

Setting a firm priority and establishing these boundaries made my mental health easier to maintain. I was not constantly torn in conflicting directions. This is not to say all tension and stress were eliminated, but they were greatly reduced and easier to manage.

When it all came down to it I preferred to earn less and have more flexible time. I also preferred to pay higher salaries for good staff in the office and at home, because surrounding myself with good people made my life so much easier and helped me to be more effective (and much nicer). These were conscious choices and good ones. A good team both in the office and at home is an investment in your future, not an expense. Being clear and communicating your boundaries to both your family and the people with whom you work are key actions.

In the long run, did those choices help or hurt my career? Did they hinder my long-term earning capability? I'll never know. I was comfortable with my choice, no matter what.

- How are you investing in your future?

Lessons Learned

- Sitting at home crying or feeling dissatisfied will not solve a problem or bring opportunities to you.
- Getting back into the workforce is an investment in your future.
- If you want to get a job, talk to people, find out what is going on.
- If you want to get out of your house, then you have to actually get out of your house.
- Prepare for an interview thoroughly, practice, and know the issues.
- Know the job's salary range.
- Know and be clear about your personal priorities.
- Have a vision for your organization.
- You can choose your stress.
- Invest in top staff. It is not an expense; *it is an investment.*
- Invest in secure and stable child care, delegate.
- Get an attractive business wardrobe.
- *Remember:* Other women may not always be rooting for you.

Thus, the product of an idealized design is not an ideal state or system, but an ideal-seeking state or system.

—Russell L. Ackoff, *The Art of Problem Solving*

Opportunities Really Are Everywhere

In this chapter, you'll discover

- how to create a movement;
- how to define your idea and turn it into reality;
- how to shape a constituency;
- how to build a board of directors/advisors;
- how to raise money;
- how to grow step by step; and
- the importance of good questions.

Being so passionate about architecture and its importance in our lives, I talk about it to anyone and everyone, anywhere I can. One evening at a small dinner party for local historic preservation, I sat next to a quiet and unassuming man named Otto. Of course I started talking about the importance of architecture. He was very receptive to my ideas, especially those on teaching children about architecture and city planning. After all, we agreed, these children are the future members of the city planning commission, the historic commission, and the zoning board.

Otto asked many questions. Since he appeared so interested, I kept in touch with him. Later I learned that he was a very generous philanthropist in the Philadelphia region and cared deeply about the quality of his city. We met several times, and each time he would ask questions about my vision for the city and a civic organization to influence its buildings, parks, and urban spaces.

He never expressed his opinion but just kept asking questions.

Who will direct this organization?

- How will the public participate?
- What will be your programs' relationship with the public school leadership?
- How will the architecture community participate?
- What kind of board are you thinking about?
- How can your organization effectively influence decisions and choices that affect quality of life in this city?
- Are you looking at models in other cities? What do you admire?
- What has not worked?

His pertinent questions helped me clarify my thinking and ultimately guided my strategies to make this civic organization happen.

I wanted to create an organization that represented the public's concerns about issues pertaining to the architecture and planning of their city. It would include a civic forum to discuss important research and theories about urban design. We would have a docent-led architecture tour program to raise interest in the architectural treasures of the city and neighborhoods. We would capitalize on the architecture of the city to promote tourism. We would develop a program from kindergarten through twelfth grade in as many schools as possible, using architecture as a way to teach history, math, reading, physics, and other subjects.

During this time, I was working as the executive director of the Philadelphia chapter of the AIA. The institute's focus is to provide resources for architects in Philadelphia. This entirely new nonprofit organization's goal was to serve the public by being a civic forum for issues of architecture and urban elements. My vision statement was clear, concise, and well organized: a paragraph about each program that would make up the activities of the nonprofit. What the vision statement lacked, however, were paragraphs about who would lead it and how this Foundation for Architecture start-up would be funded.

Each time Otto and I spoke, he was very enthusiastic and asked the same question: "But who will run this new organization?"

And I, being naïve, would answer the same way each time: "Oh, I will find someone!"

And he would say, "Aren't *you* interested?"

And I would say, "But I already have a job, as director of the AIA."

This conversation went on for a year.

Finally, upon returning from a trip to Los Angeles invigorated by the can-do spirit there, I called Otto to report, "In L.A. they look for ways to make an idea happen. Here in Philadelphia they look for reasons why it can't be done. I'm tired of that attitude. I would like to run this new organization. I want to make it happen."

Without hesitation Otto said, "Well, I've decided to fund it. I'll come to your office, and you can tell me what you need."

I was speechless. I began to realize that Otto invested in people, not just ideas. With his approach of questioning but offering no opinion, I discovered, he had been patiently waiting for me, on my own, in my own time frame, to move toward this decision when I was fully committed and ready. He had been the CEO of a major international chemical company, and he and his family had created several philanthropic foundations.

That was the first of many such discussions, each resulting in increasingly larger amounts and, even more important, the start of a close friendship with an extraordinary person. The initial membership contribution of seventy-five dollars was only the beginning. Through his foundations, the organization and my salary were supported for many years.

He also taught me to listen more carefully to good questions and not to jump in immediately with my opinion (which I do far too often). He was an unusual combination of kindness, modesty, and gentle influence. He possessed incredible insight and a keen intellect. And he had a delightful sparkle in his eyes.

He taught me that if you want to do something, commit 100 percent to it, take the chance, and get on with it—make it happen—that is, after you have thought it through! And have a clear enough plan to carry out the vision. After all, as the idea is implemented the organization will evolve. Have the courage to step forward!

World-renowned architects Denise Scott Brown and Robert Venturi
join me in support for the Foundation for Architecture.

Leslie Gallery-Dilworth

Building Leverage and Shaping a Coalition

With Otto's initial contribution I structured a plan to leverage his support by having his contribution matched from other sources. With these matches his initial commitment of $60,000 would become $180,000. This established a commitment, an involvement, and a stable revenue source for three years—enough time to launch the Foundation for Architecture.

With an initial resource of $2,800, a staff of one-half person (me), and Otto's seed money, over the next five years we grew to a staff of eighteen, with a docent-led architecture guide program of seventy. Our Architecture in the Schools program was active in more than seventy-five K-12 schools in the region, financed by the public school system, grants, and the volunteer time of architects and architecture students. This program used architecture as a way to teach many subjects, among them math, history, social studies, sciences, and language. The program and the workbooks became a model for similar programs across the country and received recognition from the president of the United States and even from the United Nations! We also published a beautifully designed guidebook to the city and its architecture that is still being reprinted and updated today, thirty years later.

To generate great ideas for the city of Philadelphia, we created an international design competition funded by an international building materials manufacturer. Many of the ideas from this competition, the Certainteed Award for City Visions, have now been implemented by other organizations. We also published *City Sites,* a monthly newspaper for the public.

These important concepts of coalition building and leverage are evident in each program. We did not have power or great financial resources, but our credibility and coalition building bought us considerable influence. We were always very generous in our recognition and appreciation for the many volunteers and extraordinary staff who together made all these programs thrive.

The Beaux Arts Ball attracted 6,000 costumed partygoers.
This event provided all operating funds for Philadelphia's
Foundation for Architecture programs. Each year
included a design competition to create free-standing
pavilions that contained ornaments for partygoers.

For general operating funds, always the most difficult to raise, we created an annual fund-raising costume ball. The ball was held each year in an unfinished building to show off examples of good architecture around the city. Each year it was held in a different building, always one that was under construction. It all would have been so much easier in a hotel. So that young people could afford to attend, the tickets were carefully priced. The pricing also included another tier: an elaborate sit-down dinner for sponsors. The ball became so popular that within five years 1,200 were attending the sit-down dinner, and another 4,000 arrived later to attend the ball. Before the ball I actually saw people scalping tickets.

Having implemented all the projects from my initial vision of the organization and having a terrific team in place, including an excellent board of directors, it was time for me to leave. I thought the organization needed a different kind of person at the helm. At that point my thoughts for my future were very fuzzy. I just knew I was getting restless and that it was time to leave.

A major donor, the director of a corporate foundation, asked me, "Do you want this to be a 'Leslie project' that dissipates when you move on, or do you want it to be an institution in the city?" He went on to say, "Neither is right and neither is wrong. But you have to make a choice, because that will change how you build the Foundation for Architecture in the future. You are the senior person, but there is no depth in the leadership at this time. If you want it to be an institution, you need to bring in a different type of person, and more senior people." So that's exactly what I did.

An organization goes through "passages," just as a person does. Some people are excellent in the beginning, with frequent and direct access to the founder, but they cannot adjust to a larger, more structured organization in which they must share the founder's attention. Other people function much better in a more structured environment. Staffing needs to evolve. And so too did my needs. Yours will as well.

Not-for-Profit Is a Tax Status, Not a State of Mind

One day while interviewing a recent graduate from a master's program in nonprofit management, I asked what she thought was the difference between managing a for-profit and a not-for-profit organization. She said, "In managing a for-profit you manage the revenues and profits. In a not-for-profit you manage the deficits."

Wrong, wrong, wrong! I told her we had never operated at a deficit and would not. A wise real estate developer and chairman of our board taught me that if you plan just to break even, you will always have a deficit! That is definitely not a way to run any business, especially a not-for-profit.

When I stepped down from the Foundation for Architecture, the organization was operating on an annual budget of $2.5 million, with no deficit.

- Do you believe in yourself?
- What chances are you willing to take?

Lessons Learned

- Raising funds and having a vision are not sufficient. You must build a broad coalition of people who support the organization and its goals, by having different types of programs for different interests, and by showing that your actions and activities do make a difference. Leverage any and all support, financial and otherwise.

- You need a carefully selected and dedicated board that, in addition to attending regular board meetings, meets annually at a structured retreat to advise or coach the director and staff. When you have a power-packed board, you absolutely want to encourage the best of their thinking. They do not want to listen to a lot of reports that they can just read on their own time. Any board requires nurturing and attention. That is the responsibility of the executive director or CEO.

  I liked to select our future board members from the executives who would be the next generation of leaders, rather than the current top dog. When these future leaders rose to the top, they would remember and continue to support us.

- One report to which the board, CEO, and staff must heed is the financial report, and the CEO/director must emphasize this. I always thought of the financial report and the budget as a design. Instead of lines, we were using numbers; instead of rooms, we were creating programs. In any business, numbers are your friends.

- Build a strong staff. The staff is the team that will carry out programs and generate fresh ideas. Surround yourself with very bright, energetic, and challenging people; pay them the best you can possibly pay them; and reward them with the luxury of trying their new ideas, enabling them to reach beyond what they thought they were capable of achieving. High turnover is a sign of a dysfunctional organization. When good people can grow with you, they do not need to go elsewhere.

Our programs and visions provided an opportunity for people, companies, and foundations to become involved. If you have a compelling vision, why wouldn't they want to become involved? Of course, the opportunity has to be a win-win, so I always ask, "What interests you about this? How would you see this idea developing?" (I ask this even if they have not expressed any interest.) Asking is an invitation to engage the funder or potential donor in a discussion. This initiates their thinking about it. When you find yourself doing all the talking, that is a red flag. Stop.

- Try to have a personal friend or business associate who has leverage set up the fund-raising appointment. He or she does not have to say a thing except for the introduction.

Radiating enthusiasm and being knowledgeable about your vision is like a magnet. People will want to be involved if you show how it benefits them as well.

- Many people are reluctant to ask for money or donations. Personally, I like to raise funds, which is different from asking for a handout.
- Don't start an expensive program unless you have funding in place. This holds true for both a for-profit business and a not-for-profit organization.

The Foundation for Architecture grew from a staff of one
person, part-time, to a staff of eighteen in four years.

I believe life is a series of near misses. A lot of what we ascribe to luck is not luck at all. It's seizing the day and accepting responsibility for your future. It's seeing what other people don't see and pursuing that vision.

—Howard Schultz, founder of Starbucks Coffee

When and How Is It Time
for You to Move On

In this chapter, you will discover

- how to recognize the best use of your skills and talents;
- when to transition;
- how to define and structure your new venture;
- how to go from vague idea to proposal; and
- what this will cost.

Dream up something, make it happen, get it going smoothly, and then leave—that is what I like to do even when I do not know what comes next. I am not suggesting you do the same, but rather, for you to know in which areas you are most effective.

Over lunch one day I mentioned this to my philanthropist friend Otto. He asked me what I would like to do next. He said, "Write it down, no more than a page with a budget, and I will look at it." His request was the first step in designing my plan for the next phase of my life!

Although I was incubating some thoughts about my future, they were not fully formed. What was my vision *for me*? Writing it down is essential. Adding a price tag and timeline is essential to making it real. Now I had an invitation to think through my ideas more thoroughly.

When you are running a growing organization, it often takes all your energy to keep it going. There is very little energy left over or time to think, to create, to envision. My thoughts for my future beyond the foundation had been nebulous until I began using a design framework to look at where I would ideally like to be (the "vision" and "ideal" steps) and, realistically, where I was (the "mess" step) and then identifying the steps in between.

Again over lunch he scrutinized my proposal. My concept was to fund the one year of transition in leadership for the Foundation for Architecture, and it laid out the following two years of my life. It covered two years to travel, take some courses, and think. (The estimated budget request was for several hundred thousand dollars.) Before I allowed "the impossible" voice in my head to speak aloud, I wrote out my ideal in words. We have all heard that inner voice saying, "No, it will not happen."

For me this proposed plan was the ideal. I thought the ideal would be a starting point for an exploratory discussion. After a few questions, he said it looked reasonable, and that he would fund it.

Again, I was astonished, but to Otto my plan was a worthwhile investment.

He invested in people—people who could accomplish good things for the city of Philadelphia, to which he was very committed.

Colleagues and friends later commented to me, "What luck!" This was definitely not luck. Good fortune, yes, but not luck. He had funded my visions before, and I had delivered.

You must be willing to define your ideal, for then it might really happen.

At a dinner party I overheard Otto telling the people across from him, "The Foundation for Architecture has been the most successful investment I have ever made. And it was such a modest amount." To him it was such a small amount of money, but to me his financial support and commitment to my vision were huge.

Years later, as he was dying, I visited him often. On one of my visits, I gathered my courage to tell him how important he had been to me and how much I valued his guidance, his financial support, and his confidence.

He replied, "No, it is I who want to thank you. You have given me great pleasure in being able to help you create your visions and to be a part of their success. Thank you for the joy you have brought me."

Once again, Otto introduced me to a different way of thinking.

Otto's gentle questions and insights were so valuable. Every city should be so fortunate. Every community needs an Otto.

It all began at a dinner, fifteen years earlier. Dinners can be about much more than dining! Breakfasts, lunches, and dinners are opportunities! (I always order and eat dessert. Nothing interferes with that.)

- With whom are you going to dinner?
- Will you chat with the person sitting next to you?

Lessons Learned

- It is important to recognize when it's time to move on.
- Move on!
- Define your dream or ideal. Write it down your "preferred future". Define the steps. Estimate the costs.

A pessimist sees the difficulty in every opportunity; an optimist sees the opportunity in every difficulty.

—Winston Churchill

A Big Problem for Everyone Else Can Be an Even Bigger Opportunity for You

In this chapter, you'll discover

- how to recognize that the " someone else" sometimes is *you;*
- how small-scale interventions can lead to larger, more effective actions;
- how to talk their language;
- that naysayers can be your allies;
- how to gain consensus; and
- the importance of looking at the system rather than just the parts.

"Someone [Else] Should Do Something about This!"

When is the last time you were confused by street signs? When sign systems work well, you do not even notice them. But when they fail, you can end up in the city dump—as my husband and I once did returning from the airport to our home in Philadelphia ... oddly enough, the city where we had both lived our entire adult lives.

Returning from a vacation in Spain, we followed new overhead interstate signs and took a wrong exit. We literally wound up in front of a barbed-wire gate with a sign that proclaimed "City Dump. No Admission." This may sound humorous now, but at the time it was as outrageous as it was frustrating. How could we get lost driving home from our airport? We had driven home from the airport many times, but this time we had followed the recently installed signs.

We had driven around Spain for several weeks, and neither of us spoke Spanish. We were never lost. Navigation there was simple. Signs throughout the country were legible, with understandable symbols and consistent color coding and names.

Now, appalled at our situation and contemplating the dump, I exclaimed, "If *we* can get lost, what happens to visitors or people who don't speak English? Why doesn't someone correct this? This is a big problem. Someone should do something!" (Notice the bland, third-person approach here, the noncommittal approach, turning this responsibility over to the infamous "someone else.")

I'll bet you have said the same thing: "Someone should do something about this!" How many times have you noticed a problem, complained for a moment, and then moved on? How many times have you allowed this kind of opportunity to slip by?

We have all done this. Next time, be aware that this problem may be an opportunity for you—*step one*!

As director of the Foundation for Architecture, a civic interest group, I was at least in a position to bring this situation to the attention of the powers that be in the city of Philadelphia. From the director of the streets department, to the convention and visitors bureau, to the mayor's office, the response was the same. Each person shrugged their shoulders and said, "There's nothing I can do. It is too complicated. It is someone else's fault. It is someone else's responsibility."

In other words, they had other priorities. It became evident that signs were no one's priority, so I made them mine. But what could I actually do?

I may not have been in a position of power to make a change happen, but at least I could bring this to the attention of the movers and shakers who *could* make something happen. At least I could orchestrate a symposium to bring attention to this problem. I was sure that someone else would pick up this issue and take it on if they were just more aware of the situation and the opportunity. We titled the symposium "Can Image Be Substance?" (This title appealed to the audience and was provocative but not offensive.)

The president of Mellon Bank agreed to host the event on the bank's elegant executive reception floor, overlooking City Hall. Invitations were extended under his name and that of Mellon Bank. "The Foundation for Architecture" was in very small type and hardly noticeable. My name appeared nowhere, since it meant little to anyone invited to this symposium. I personally prepared the invitation list, including all the bigwigs from tourism, business, government, philanthropy, and arts and culture. Anyone who could keep a solution from happening was invited, as well as any institution or business affected by signage.

Our objective was to inspire this audience—people who had the resources to change the signage—to want to bring about this change. An outstanding panel of experts from around the country presented successful examples of how other cities and organizations approached this type of challenge. Senior executives always like to know what is happening elsewhere, especially if it includes positive solutions.

Knowing the tenured head of the streets department would think this was of no concern to him (yes, that is right), I invited him to make the introductory remarks and sit at the head table with the panel. That way he had to attend and could not leave early.

He had to come to his own awareness that positive change could happen.

As a city bureaucrat, he could then get some credit for being a leader. Bludgeoning would not work; it never does. After the program I noticed him approaching one of the panelists from out of town, making arrangements to meet and to visit this other city.

Turnout was excellent, because no one wanted to offend the president of the bank by not attending. I thought that would be the end of my involvement. I was sure that someone else would take charge of this challenge.

The president of one of the city's two major philanthropic foundations asked me to submit a proposal to him to carry this initiative forward. A week later I submitted a modest proposal for three or four more forums such as the one we had just had. The proposed budget was $30,000. Again I thought that someone else attending one of these forums would pick up this initiative and take it on.

After reading my proposal, the president of the foundation said, "This is not what I meant. If you really wanted to make systemic and long-term change happen, what would you do?"

What a profound and provocative question. I knew nothing about signs, except that many of those in Philadelphia were useless. I replied that I would have to go away and think about it. That is exactly what I did.

That question posed a wonderful challenge—an exhilarating opportunity to reach into a complex problem and design a solution based on a systems-wide approach. Not only did I not know much about signs, I knew nothing about the systems and the components: the legislation, regulation, management, funding, maintenance, and politics. I actually thought this was exciting.

The Language of Pink Flamingoes

About this time, I heard the city was releasing a request for proposals to improve the signage in the downtown core, and they were inviting only engineers to submit proposals. I asked to be included in the meeting, which included street and traffic engineers and the head of the convention and visitors bureau, but no graphic designers. They thought there was no harm in including me, as this was clearly an engineering problem and had nothing to do with design or architecture. So how could I interfere with their agenda? After all, I only ran a small, upstart organization with no real power to effect change.

Each time I brought up the issue of including designers, they politely ignored me and continued with their discussion. At last I started listening more carefully to the language they were using. After a while I interrupted and said, "I am talking about an integrated public information system." (Engineers like the words *integrated, information,* and *system.*) At that point one of the engineers exclaimed, "Oh, why didn't you say that before? You kept talking about design and designers. I thought you meant we should put a few pink flamingoes on the big green interstate signs. Every time you mentioned the word *design,* I translated that to mean big bucks, expensive signs, and fluff in our budget."

The lesson I learned that day was that to be understood and make an impact, first listen carefully, and then, to be heard, use the other's language. *Design* was not a good word to these folks. For me it had always been a word meaning good things. Clearly, it did not have the same connotation with this audience. When I used their language, they readily understood. That was a major "aha" moment for me.

Sometimes It Is So Broken You Just Have to Start Over (A Systems Approach)

Sometimes a situation is just so bad that it cannot be solved piecemeal. Rather, you have to look at it from high above and design what would be the perfect solution as if nothing existed before. In this case it would mean rethinking the entire sign system in the city, region, and state, not just the downtown signs.

Step one would be to look at the entire existing situation—the *mess*, as organizational theorist Dr. Russell L. Ackoff of the Wharton School at Penn would call it. For this project, what I called the "existing big mess" included all departments, agencies, cultural attractions, regulations, legislation, and budgets. Signage was only the manifestation of a deeper, more complex malfunctioning system.

I had a hidden agenda as well: to prove that good design would cost not more but actually less if properly planned. This was the first step toward addressing a permanent and long-term solution for the city and region, for a comprehensive integrated public information system (more commonly known as street signs).

The proposal for "Direction Philadelphia" was for $980,000 (in 1985 dollars) over a three-year period. This did not even include any physical signs—just a few prototypes!

The president of the foundation read it while I sat there. Then and there he looked up and said, "Fine. We will fund this." I was speechless ... speechless and frightened. I had never done anything like this, nor had I ever received a grant of this magnitude.

It is okay to be scared for a moment. After that, you have to move on. Do not let being scared, or the fact that you have not done something before, stop you. Just get on with it. Just make it work. Give it the best of your thinking and the best of your energy! You do not have time to be scared.

For me this positive response was great and not so great. Now I actually had to take this idea to reality and do it. I could not fail; too much was riding on this.

Coalition Building

How do you create a team of support for an idea? Collaboration!

First we identified everyone who would be affected positively by this initiative, and then we made a list of anyone who could keep this idea from happening.

In addition to the heads of departments and agencies, we included the political appointees; but because political appointees come and go, we invited middle-ranking staff. Middle-ranking employees with tenure could easily place any of the recommendations in the "round file," never to be seen again. They could and would outwait the elected and appointed administrators. If we wanted long-term change, they had to buy into this. Our project had to be theirs as well.

Ninety stakeholders participated in the process. From the beginning I set the policy that as a group we would only make unanimous recommendations—not even by majority vote. Everyone had to agree. Of course, more experienced voices said that would never happen. But it did.

I explained to the stakeholders that the Foundation for Architecture was just the facilitator. Direction Philadelphia belonged to them, the stakeholders.

Shaping the Ideal

To get everyone on the same page, we started with the premise that the first step was to establish mutual respect and tolerance for others' priorities and perspectives. This we did by asking each person to prepare a presentation on their major concerns and the elements of their ideal system. Second, we worked on the premise that everyone wanted to do "the right thing." (Sometimes they just didn't know what that was.) And third, we agreed that everyone's opinion was as valuable as the next person's.

Once we collected ninety individual ideals, the group synthesized this information into one that everyone could recommend. This was the collective *ideal.*

We had analyzed all the existing expenditures having to do with street signs from all the different agencies at the local, state, and federal levels. The sum of existing expenditures was critical; this would be our maximum budget. Our target was to develop a comprehensive system that would cost considerably less than the existing one. For credibility we hired consultants from Penn's Wharton School of Business to conduct this analysis.

Another objective was to reform the regulations. We identified each issue. For instance, long-term maintenance and management would certainly be a significant roadblock. A dedicated funding source would be essential. In the scheme of things for a large city, how important, really, is signage next to, say, emergency medical services?

Naturally, I cared the most about designing the signs. I had to work through all of the contributing factors first. The Los Angeles design firm Sussman Prezja participated in the process from day one. I had chosen the firm myself. That was the one major decision I made myself, because I did not want to trust it to a committee. In the end the designers would be responsible for what the public would actually see.

With all this information in hand (that is, the description of the *mess* and the absolute *ideal*), and with all the stakeholders digesting it together, we moved to the next step.

Design a Doable Ideal

After taking the ninety ideals and synthesizing them into one, we literally meshed the mess with the synthesized ideal to develop the *doable ideal*. This would be our doable vision and our goal. From where we were to where we wanted to be, we identified the steps. Remember: we were still not talking about what the signs would look like; we were just talking about the revised underlying support system as agreed upon by the ninety stakeholders. But we finally had an accurate picture of our city's signage mess, and we knew where we wanted to end up—and now we knew how to get there.

A Constituency for Change: A Solid Foundation

This was not enough. Many cities install a sign system. But how many of these last for almost thirty years? Here is the secret.

While all this was going on, we were building a constituency for change. We were building a substantial ongoing support group. It was never seen as my personal project. Nor was it seen as the Foundation for Architecture's project. It was the project of Direction Philadelphia. And who and what was Direction Philadelphia? The ninety stakeholders and the organizations, businesses, and people they represented. At one of the regular stakeholder meetings, someone referred to Direction Philadelphia as the Foundation's project. From that meeting on, I invited this person to sit at the facilitator's table in the front of the room, while I sat in the back of the room. This way he would realize that this project was as much his as anyone else's there. Image *can* be substance, even in the smallest way.

In complex community projects such as this, the shortest route is often not the most direct. Often the route that should take the least time ends up taking the most time. We may have appeared to be zigzagging, but we were building a strong, long-term constituency for change and success. This constituency would truly represent the community and would continue to support this program long the original stakeholders and I were no longer involved.

The Direction Philadelphia system is now in its thirtieth year. Clearly, the doable ideal continues to be done.

Partnering with the Press: Public Support and Enthusiasm

While the technical aspects of the project were progressing, we were orchestrating a citywide public enthusiasm campaign. Our intention was to create awareness and dissatisfaction with the current state of signs in a humorous way, not by criticizing or blaming any one public agency or individual. We enlisted the newspapers and all the TV stations by encouraging reporters to follow the existing signs to see where they would end up! This was so much fun for the reporters that for several months it became a regular, one-minute feature on the evening news.

If this effort had been superficial, and if I had been the only one cheerleading the effort to change the system, the bureaucrats would have patiently waited for the next administration or for me to fall out of favor, and the entire project would have collapsed. But since we involved the entrenched bureaucrats by showing them honest respect, their voices and their opinions had real weight. (Remember Lyndon Johnson's eloquent "I would rather have my enemies in the tent pissing out, than outside pissing in.")

Direction Philadelphia is no longer limited to Center City. It extends throughout all city neighborhoods and into the surrounding region. Direction Philadelphia is now managed by the Philadelphia Center City District, a business improvement district.

- Is there a big problem where you live that you could help solve? Yes! ... and you could! Just get started.

Directing people around the city, Direction Philadelphia is now
in its thirtieth year. Pictured here with me is designer Deborah
Sussman of Sussman Prejza. A proud moment in 1992.

Lessons Learned

- Keep in mind the things that annoy you and what you'd want someone else to change for you. Then forget someone else doing it, and do it yourself!
- Think about the system and all its interrelated parts, not just the tip of the iceberg.
- Think big.... Now think even bigger.
- Identify everyone who can be positively or negative impacted by this problem.
- Begin by enlisting the support of those who can keep your idea or project from happening. Listen to their concerns.
- Keep your name out of the paper, and stand at the back of the room.
- Don't bludgeon; be smarter and use psychology or humor.
- Always know who will pay for the project and how it will be maintained for the long run.
- Elected officials and appointees come and go, but tenured bureaucrats are very patient and can wait it out.
- Listen to the language they are using; speak *their* language.
- Even signage can be fun and important.

Management is doing things right; leadership is doing the right things.

—Peter Drucker

Rebuilding an Organization That Has Lost Its Way

In this chapter, you will discover

- how to look for financial clues;
- how to deal with legal concerns;
- quick steps to new revenue opportunities; and
- the importance of a board retreat.

One day out of the blue, I received a call from a professional acquaintance who was a well-respected and successful environmental graphic designer. Environmental graphic designers develop identity and branding programs, complex signage, and way-finding systems for cities, campuses, healthcare facilities, shopping malls, and airports (and other transit systems), and interpretive exhibitions for museums. I became aware of this field and this organization when I was CEO of the Foundation for Architecture, designing the Direction Philadelphia project. SEGD (the Society for Environmental Graphic Design) was a small but respected organization with a loyal membership of designers from fields including graphic design, architecture, industrial design, landscape architecture, interior design, and branding.

Over breakfast one day, the past president of the organization explained that SEGD needed an executive director. They had been unsuccessful in their previous two attempts and would like some advice. The board was unaware of the extent of their financial problems. The board had not been asking the right questions. The organization had never done an audit by a independent auditor.

I told her what I thought the organization could become and what they should *not* look for. My observation was that this field was at the confluence of many growing design disciplines, including branding, information architecture, and storytelling through exhibition design. The potential for growth was huge. It was a vital, exciting time for those in this field.

Unfortunately, most of them did not realize this. They were trying to limit the membership and to become recognized as a profession; however, there was no educational requirement and no licensing or registration body, so, in my opinion, it was difficult to be considered a real profession.

I suggested that this organization should recognize the value of its diversity and potential expansion, rather than focus on its exclusivity and limitations. Its members simply did not realize that their field was at the juncture of so many rich opportunities. They were thinking about hiring someone whose primary credential would be to accept a low salary. Such short-sighted thinking! That might be a big mistake, as they might just get what they paid for.

I offered to look over their financial statements but also said, very firmly, that there was absolutely no way I would ever again work with another not-for-profit membership organization whose major challenges were fund-raising and financial insecurity. I had done that for years, and I was ready for the for-profit world.

In reviewing the financial statements, I realized the organization was actually financially bankrupt but with the right leadership could be vibrant, successful, and influential. For me, sitting in my garden pondering the possibilities, this was becoming a challenging design problem. They had no money and substantial debt, but they would receive dues. They also had a loyal membership base that included some of the best and most influential designers in the world. And the organization was very respected.

SEGD programs could have bigger and more influential conferences that could produce substantial revenue. They could produce outstanding publications and, with the professional development education curriculum that could be developed, SEGD might become a first-rate education provider.

I could feel myself becoming excited about the kinds of programs that could be developed under the aegis of SEGD. This could be a great opportunity for both the organization, the members and for me. This could be so much fun; it would not be just a job.

But first I had to figure out what I would require as compensation for my time, expertise, efforts, and leadership—and ultimately their success. It had to be a win-win. If I wanted this to happen, then I had to design a proposal and compensation package to submit to them. But they had no financial resources at that moment. And I was living in Philadelphia, while their office was in Washington, D.C.

Build your life on possibilities, not the limitations.

There is always a way. My four-step plan would offer a good road map for the organization, and for me. I designed a plan for SEGD that would be my ideal, meet my needs, and cost them no more than they were currently planning to pay an executive director. This plan was also ideal for SEGD. It would be a win-win.

For years SEGD had been run like a hobby. If they wanted to be successful, SEGD needed to be run like a business. We would begin drafting a business plan. To access their commitment to change, I proposed a two-day working retreat, which I would lead, with the national board coming to Philadelphia. The other purposes of the retreat were to draw out their visions for the future, identify the current state of the field, and place a price on what it would cost to get to their as-yet-undetermined ultimate goal.

What a challenging and rewarding two days! What we learned became the road map for creating a reborn organization. So the board could see that I knew what I was doing and could lead them to a greater success than they had envisioned, I introduced them to the Foundation for Architecture. It was also vital that the board members understand this was a serious business, so I also introduced them to an outstanding attorney who specialized in nonprofit law. A not-for-profit is a serious business, and their decisions had legal consequences.

Many boards say they want to develop a successful organization, but they are not prepared to take the actions required, nor are they prepared to give the CEO the power required. They want to hold the CEO accountable but do not give the CEO enough flexibility, authority, or respect. Absolutely, boards should not micromanage! If boards think they have to micromanage, either the executive director or the board should be replaced.

We followed my four-step process to

1. identify the problem;
2. shape the ideal vision;
3. determine where we are (the mess); and
4. develop a very specific road map to get from here to there (including dollars, staffing, and timeline).

We envisioned opening up the organization to many overlapping disciplines, rather than narrowing the definition of the field. But the very first priorities were economic stability in the long run and stopping the hemorrhaging in the short run. If I did well for them (which, after the retreat with the board, I was certain I could do), they would do well, and I would be compensated appropriately. They had absolutely nothing to lose, as their alternative was to dissolve. It is always good to take over a defunct or teetering-on-the-brink organization, as the board will usually be very supportive of change and willing to make decisions quickly. With our road map in place and updated annually, the organization grew from a hobby to a serious business.

An organization must have adequate revenues to provide services to its members, pay the staff competitively, and be relevant to the public. Again, a nonprofit is only a tax status; it is not a state of mind. We had the organization in the black at the end of the first year. Twelve years later, with stable finances in place, a reserve fund, and an excellent staff of seven, together we had created and implemented all of the programs outlined at the initial retreat.

Ever wonder who designs signage in airports? Museums? Hospitals? Shopping malls? SEGD, Society for Environmental Graphic Design, is an international organization for designers who shape experiences through way-finding, identity and exhibit design. This is our SEGD administrative team.

What matters is that the goals are achieved, not the number of days worked. What also should matter is that the goals are reached, not that the staff has to be in the same room at the same time. This approach required putting together a team of people who did not need their hands held and liked to work independently but could also cooperate. We had three people in the headquarters in Washington, D.C.; I was in Philadelphia (and later Galisteo, New Mexico); and others were in Philadelphia and Ohio. It worked well. Because of the quality of our staff and our board, and modern technology, I was able to reduce the time I physically spent in the Washington office from three days each week to one week a month.

The most important decision the board makes is the hiring of the executive director. As board membership rotates, so too do their insights and strengths. A volunteer board is like a garden of plants that have to be nurtured. It is the executive director's job to water, fertilize, and nurture the plants so that this garden blossoms.

Both a for-profit business and a not-for-profit require a strong, visionary leader as CEO, one who gives great respect to the finances, budgets, income, and expenses! The answer is not always to cut expenses. Sometimes the answer is to manage expenses while simultaneously increasing revenue and programs and thinking bigger, not smaller.

The CEO must have the strength and diplomacy to keep the board on the right track. Otherwise, each board member may want to have his or her favorite program implemented. That may be good for that board member, but not good for the entire organization. Being a good board member takes training. Being on a board is very different from being the boss of your own company.

- Are you overlooking a potential win-win opportunity?

Lessons Learned

- The right CEO at the right time can make an enormous difference in creating a healthy organization or in destroying the organization. The board can do the same.
- A small nonprofit (or any business) is extremely fragile. Each programmatic and financial decision can have critical repercussions.
- The board and staff are partners; forget the concept of board setting policy and staff implementing it.
- Staff does not all have to be in one office, in the same location.
- Staff is an extraordinary resource that the board should value and reward.
- Hire very smart people who have drive and are caring; enlist board members with the same attributes.
- Always, always, always respect the bottom line and the budget.
- When the going gets tough, sometimes it is time to expand, not retreat; cutting expenses is not the only possible strategy.
- Nurture and appreciate the board; they are volunteering their time.
- Annual review of the strategic plan and tallying accomplishments keeps everyone on the same page, and focused.
- Hire to compensate for your weaknesses, not to duplicate your strengths. Don't be intimidated by working with people smarter than you. It's a very smart thing to do!

One recognizes one's course by discovering the paths that stray from it.

—Albert Camus

A Few Detours

In this chapter, you'll discover

- why be alert to fear of failure, and
- that there is something to learn wherever you are.

Until my senior year in college, I was always very directed. I knew where I wanted to go and how to get there. I had a plan. I had a design for my life. From the time I was ten, I wanted to be an architect. This was at a time when women did not become architects. In fact, at that time women were expected to go to a good college, find a good husband, and stay home and raise children.

Nevertheless, my parents were 100 percent supportive of my becoming an architect and never tried to dissuade me. My dad always told me I could be or do whatever I wanted to. And so I did—until I was a senior in college. Then I became a little confused or cowardly.

I applied to many graduate programs and many schools. At Harvard I applied to their masters programs in the history of art, in architecture, and in landscape architecture. As if that were not sufficient, I applied to the Yale graduate program in medieval studies, the graduate program in history of art at NYU, and the master of landscape architecture program at the University of Pennsylvania in Philadelphia.

But I always wanted to be an architect. So what was happening here? Was I afraid of failure? Was I *just plain afraid?*

To assure that I would not have to make a decision or a commitment, I neglected to complete any of the applications, and of course I received a nice postcard from each school and each program reminding me that they could not make a decision unless I submitted one more minor form that would make my application complete. (Of course, this must have been by my subconscious design.)

My college advisor at Penn, a noted art historian who had graciously written those many letters of recommendation for me, said, "Leslie, if only you could get both feet in the same pot at the same time, you could be very successful!" (Little did he realize that not doing so would ultimately be my strength!)

After graduating from college, not having completed any of the applications and therefore not having been accepted at any of the schools (but not having been rejected either), I did what was then the standard and required route for bright women liberal arts graduates from Ivy League schools: I went to secretarial school for a month. For a young woman at the time, secretarial skills were essential to getting an entry-level position anywhere.

I flunked shorthand and received the lowest possible acceptable passing grade in typing.

Armed with my secretarial degree, I went off to New York City. My poor secretarial skills kept me from getting past the gatekeepers in human resources departments. But I persevered, and finally, after many rejections, I was hired.

My First Real Job! A Secretary

I flunked the typing test by one word, but the human resources (HR) person was at her wit's end trying to find a secretary for the director of marketing research at *Good Housekeeping* magazine and Hearst Publications. The HR person said the director didn't like anyone and fired everyone, and she implied that because the director was a woman, she was a bitch. So the HR person actually said, "I have nothing to lose by sending you up to meet this woman, even if you can't type well enough."

In the interview the director of marketing research asked me only one question: "What would you say if it were three o'clock and I wasn't back from lunch yet and Mr. Hearst called for me?"

I said, "I would say that you had just stepped out of the office for a moment, and I would have you call him the minute you returned."

"Perfect," she said. "You're hired." She explained that the previous secretary actually told Mr. Hearst, who had called at three, "She is not back from lunch yet."

Then there was the typing challenge. This was all statistical typing, before the days of Wite-Out, let alone computers and copiers. I had to make six carbon copies of reports that were all columns of numbers. I am dyslexic, so I often read 6 as 9 or 9 as 6 and reversed numbers in columns. I would make so many mistakes that I didn't want anyone to see how many sheets of paper I was going through each day. I started to bring bigger and bigger purses to work. At the end of each day, I would stuff my bag with all the sheets of paper I was wasting and throw them out at home. Within a few weeks I was bringing what looked like a shopping bag!

The upside of the job was that I watched a really good female executive in action. She was the highest-ranked woman in the field. I got to taste all the food in the test kitchen, and, best of all, part of my job was to read all the magazines that Hearst published. When I was bored I cleaned out and reorganized all the director's files that hadn't been touched in five years. (Take the initiative. Don't just look busy; *be* busy.) I also paid close attention to the research they were doing, how they shaped the questions and how the questions were ordered. I asked a lot of questions myself.

I soon realized that I didn't like New York City or being a secretary. Now I knew for sure that my life wouldn't be conventional and easy. A few months of secretarial school wouldn't suffice. Sitting at a desk in someone else's office wasn't enough. I needed to buckle down and pursue my dream in a male-dominated, challenging field.

At the end of the summer, I told my boss I was leaving. She said, "I hoped you would stay a year, when I would have arranged an editorial position for you at one of the good magazines. But I want you to know that you were the best secretary I have ever had ... provided you have your own typist!"

So at end of summer, a week before the fall semester began, I called Ian McHarg, chair of the landscape architecture program at Penn, and asked if I could please join the master's program in landscape architecture. He said yes.

Lessons Learned

- Everyone should learn to type.
- There is something good to learn wherever you are.
- Sometimes common sense is more important than skill.
- Face your fears.

When I was a graduate student in Louis I. Kahn's
architecture master class at the University of Pennsylvania,
student work was reviewed by Robert Engman, sculptor, Robert
LeRicolais, French engineer, and Mr. Kahn (front left).

Mr. Kahn's classes attracted students from all over the world.
As you can see, in 1970 very few women attended architecture
school. Now most architecture schools are fifty-fifty.

When you live your life with an appreciation of coincidences and their meanings, you connect with the underlying field of infinite possibilities.

—Deepak Chopra

Coincidence Leads to Opportunity

I believe in coincidences. Do you?

Experiencing extraordinary coincidences is a thread weaving through my life.

It got me thinking ...

Why does coincidence occur more frequently to me rather than to others?

I often employ these "Four C's" with my interactions:

- curiosity
- connection/chatting
- commitment
- courage to reach out

Is coincidence the same as fate?

Is coincidence the same as synchronicity? Or luck?

You can certainly recognize coincidence, but do you take advantage of it once it has occurred? Can you encourage coincidence? Yes!

When you are open to your surroundings and observant, when you are genuinely interested in the people around you, and when you seek commonality, positive coincidences will occur. You have to invite them, by reaching out, by recognizing the potential of the encounter. Then it is up to you to recognize the coincidence and turn it into an opportunity.

How many times do you sit next to someone without consequence? How many times have you sat in an office or reception room and not looked around, oblivious to your surroundings? How often have you concluded your immediate business transaction and then departed without any conversation? Think of the potential that you might have left behind!

Here are just a few tales of some delightful, amazing, and amusing coincidences that led to remarkable opportunities in my life. Think about the coincidences in your life, opportunities you may have recognized, and those, in retrospect, you may have missed.

Opportunity and Coincidence:
Sleeping in my Dream House

Chatting

Soon after the Velvet Revolution in Czechoslovakia, I was consulting there with architects, planners, and related government agencies on the public's role in shaping the quality of the environment and making democratic planning decisions.

At one of these meetings, in Prague, while standing around chatting with a gentleman who was participating in our discussions, I mentioned that I wanted to visit the city of Brno later that week. He asked why, as most Americans do not visit Brno. I told him I wanted to see the famous Villa Tugendhat, designed by the great architect Mies van der Rohe in the early 1930s.

Because of its elegance and simplicity, it had always been my favorite modern residence. But I had only seen photos; I had never been to Brno. I explained that I did not expect to go inside, but at least I would see the exterior, and asked, "Have you seen it?"

He revealed that he was the director of the city planning department from Brno.

He then asked, "How would you like to stay there? The house is managed by my office and is used by visiting dignitaries. You can sleep there the night that you are in Brno, as long as you are out by 7:00 a.m., as the "last of the Habsburgs" is coming that day."

This was equivalent to staying at the iconic Kaufmann House, Fallingwater, designed by Frank Lloyd Wright. This was extraordinary. I could not believe my ears.

When I arrived in Brno and saw the house, it was far more spectacular than any of the photos I had seen. Imagine a sleek, white, modern, one-floor home on a street with all three-story Victorian houses. The neighbors were probably not too happy at the time it was constructed. Upon entering the house, I stood in the vestibule. My hand glided over the chrome stair rail as I descended from the entry floor to the main floor below. Soon I was looking at the famous curved rosewood wall that defined the dining area. I felt like a kid in a candy store as I savored each luxurious material.

In the early morning we arose in the absolute darkness to get dressed and prepare to leave, so the house could be readied for the arrival of the Habsburg heir. There was one problem, however. During the night the electricity had gone off. We could not see anything. Finally, I found my little travel flashlight. There we were, stumbling our way to a large, luxurious bathroom, unable to see any farther than the beam of a miniature flashlight. I held the flashlight up toward my husband's face and then toward the mirror so he could shave. We could not even use the shower because we could not see.

Daylight came and we found our way down the stairs to the dining room for breakfast. We were still laughing at the contrast between the elegant house and the lack of electricity in the bathroom. Eventually, the electricity returned and the caretakers served us breakfast. Sitting at the round wood table designed by Mies van der Rohe, with the lush rosewood wall surrounding us, we looked out the floor-to-ceiling windows onto an orchard and imagined what this house meant to the Tugendhat family. How fortunate we were to have had this rare opportunity. Unfortunately, the Tugendhat family had not been able to enjoy the house very long. Soon after the house was completed, the Nazis invaded Austria, and the Tugendhats, who were Jewish, were forced to flee.

Opportunity and Coincidence:
Prince Charles, the Italian Garden, and Me

Connection, Curiosity, and Courage

England's Prince Charles has a profound interest in architecture and garden design. He established his own school of architecture and design about twenty years ago. It focused on classical rather than contemporary architecture. At that time he had recently referred to a proposed extension to the National Gallery in London by architect Sir Richard Rodgers as a "carbuncle." This comment outraged the British architects. Most of the public agreed with the prince, and the plans were discarded. Thus began the battle between the Royal Institute of British Architects and Prince Charles. That is when Prince Charles decided to hire an architect to design and develop a new town on the classical model of an old English village. And that is when he established his own school.

I had been consulting with the Architects' Journal and some London real estate developers, attempting to mend fences between the architects and Prince Charles. In that capacity I was sitting in the lobby of St. James Palace, waiting to meet with Prince Charles's secretary. Another staff member invited me into her office to have a cup of tea while waiting. I noticed a large photo on the wall behind her. It was a high-contrast black-and-white image of a detail in a garden.

As I continued to drink my tea and look at this image, I asked her, "Is that image the garden at the Villa Lante in Italy?"

She said, "Yes, it is." I told her it was my favorite Italian Renaissance garden and villa. I said I had taught classes on landscape design and on the history and theory of landscape architecture at the University of Texas. I asked why it was on her wall. She explained that the Prince of Wales was a patron of the garden and villa and held his summer school program there. "I would love to see it in person," I said.

She responded, "Perhaps you would like to teach our landscape class this summer. It is held at the Villa Lante in Bagnaia, an hour north of Rome."

Of course ... absolutely! And then I asked, "Where are the classes actually held?"

She said, "In the Villa Lante. Under the trees in the garden, by the fountains, and in the villa's reception rooms."

Spending the days in the garden with no tourists, I thought I was living in a dream. It was a marvelous summer, with students from all over the world, and I could leisurely wander around the gardens without being glued to my camera.

At the end of the session, Prince Charles hosted an intimate dinner in the villa for the students and faculty. I was invited to sit next to him for the main course (then protocol required that I rotate to another table). He told me he was committed to preserving the villa and gardens, as well as supporting the nearby historic city of Viterbo.

Our student project in Viterbo involved working with city officials exploring a variety of solutions to integrate new structures for contemporary needs and to reuse historic structures. This was information the students from many different countries would be able to utilize as they returned to their historic cities throughout the world.

Opportunity and Coincidence:
Two Wandering Englishmen

Connections and *their* Curiosity

One winter afternoon while I was preparing to leave my office, two men entered our lobby. They were middle-aged, and conservatively but very well dressed. I was heading through our lobby with the intention of going through the door as fast as I could. Our office was in a large office building, on an upper floor, and no one had ever just wandered in. In their British accents they very politely asked, "Is this the Foundation for Architecture?"

"Yes. Why?" I responded curiously.

"Well, we are early for an appointment in this building, and on the directory in the main lobby we saw Foundation for Architecture listed. We are both very interested in architecture and wanted to know more about this organization." They explained that they were real estate developers from London and were considering some investments in Philadelphia. And then they mentioned that they were part of a group working to begin a Foundation for Architecture in London.

What a serendipitous meeting! I told them I had been consulting in London with some people who were also exploring the groundwork for a public advocacy group and an organization similar to the Philadelphia Foundation for Architecture. As soon as they mentioned the name of their firm, I realized who they were. I had been trying to meet with their partner in London. And here they were, in my office!

Because I was on my way to my kids, I offered to show them around the city and be their guide—the next day. That began a friendship and working relationship that lasted several years and opened many doors.

Opportunity and Coincidence:
Rediscovering a Childhood Friend

Connections

As director of the Foundation for Architecture, I often had conversations with public relations firms or advertising agencies that represented real estate developers or manufacturers of architectural products, to explore ways in which they might support the Foundation's activities, and the benefits to them of such a partnership.

The representative from one of these public relation firms was very interested in architecture. Periodically he mentioned a real estate developer client, but not by name. He did mention the name of the developer's public relations director and suggested that we meet. He called her Judith, but I did not recognize the last name. Then one day—a year must have gone by—he identified the firm, mentioned Judith, and this time said she was the sister of the CEO. Then I realized just who Judith was: She had been my counselor at summer camp in the Pocono Mountains when I was ten, and the president, her brother, had been kind of my friend at camp (after all, I was only a child); we had paddled canoes together, all very innocent. I had not been in touch with them since I was twelve, when both our parents chaperoned a kind of New Year's Eve date we had together in Miami Beach. And I'd had no idea that this very prominent, successful developer and real estate owner was the very boy I knew from camp parties.

Now we all renewed our friendship. George came on our board of directors and was enormously helpful. He donated to the

Foundation for Architecture by contributing office space (as in no rent) in a beautiful, historically significant building. This generously contributed space enabled the organization to expand, to have programs in the space, to increase, and to grow! Some years later I made an attempt to repay him by actively participating on the board of his favorite charity.

Opportunity and Coincidence:
The Wedding Gift to Each Other, Galisteo

Chatting and Commitment

Dick, who later became my husband, made an offer on a tract of land with a view that we both liked in Galisteo, New Mexico, about thirty miles from Santa Fe. It looked over thousands of acres of nothing: just rocks and distant mountains and high desert. The offer was refused because it was too low. That was that, we thought.

Over a year later we married, and while on our honeymoon in Santa Fe, I went into a store that I frequented on my trips there. The owner remembered me from previous visits. (I love to shop; it is my recreation, and where I do my thinking.) He asked if we had bought a property yet.

"No," I said. He asked where we wanted to be. I said Galisteo. He said his friend who was visiting from LA wanted to sell a property in Galisteo. His friend was leaving the next day, so we should contact him right away, and the storeowner handed me the name and phone number. When I returned to the hotel, I told Dick. He looked at the name, exclaiming, "This is the same person, the very same property, I made the offer on last year."

So, using my name, I called the owner. He met us the next morning, on the land. We made an offer that was less than the prior year's offer. This time it was immediately accepted, and we became the proud owners of a beautiful property, the only property we had seen throughout the state that we both really wanted.

This property, clearly meant for us, was our wedding gift to each other. It is where we now live.

When opportunities present themselves, you must act.

If we had not been in Santa Fe on that very day ...

If I had not chatted with the store owner ...

If I had not mentioned where we wanted to live ...

If we had not called the owner immediately ...

If we had not been prepared to act ...

Opportunity and Coincidence:
An English Country Cottage

Curiosity and Connections

One summer while teaching at the University of Texas, my first husband, John, and I were debating where to spend our summer vacation. It was July 4, 1976, the Bicentennial; everyone in New York City was watching the Tall Ships sail into New York Harbor. We were reading the *New York Times*. I was searching listings of houses on the East Coast for summer rentals and happened to browse, just out of curiosity, the section on European summer rentals. I read, "English Country cottage, heated swimming pool, grass tennis court, caretaker, beautiful gardens, near Oxford." The rent was less than the "little nothing" houses we had been considering on the East Coast. There was a New York telephone number. It was 7:30 a.m.

I called, just out of curiosity. The woman who answered explained that the estate was owned by an Englishman who had never rented it before and was nervous about renting it for the summer, but he was going to the south of France. She said he wanted two references and would rent only to someone who could give as a reference someone he knew personally in England, and a second reference whom she would know personally in the United States. Challenging, like a needle in a haystack, so I asked some questions.

What business was he in? He was a publisher of architectural books! Wow. I gave the name of an English author, Sir Peter

Shepheard, my former professor of architecture and landscape architecture, and my friend.

Then I asked her what business she was in, here in the States, and she also said publishing. I gave the name of friend who was founder of a publishing house. It turned out she had worked there. Clearly, this was meant to be.

I was the first to call. What a fabulous coincidence! A great house and a great summer, a wonderful experience. And, by the way, a great library.

If I had not looked at the *New York Times* on that morning, July 4, 1976 ...

If I had not ventured out of my comfort zone to explore summer rentals beyond New Jersey ...

If I had not acted by telephoning the number so early in the morning ...

If I had not asked what business the owner was in and what business the contact was in, I would have hung up and not have known whose name to give as a reference.

This was truly serendipitous.

Opportunity and Coincidence:
Looking over Her Shoulder

Curiosity and Chatting

At the time (and now, too), it was very difficult to get into a college as a transfer student, and nearly impossible to be admitted as a transfer student in a residence hall, on campus. My freshman grades were, shall we say, not that good! I thought this interview at Penn was a lost cause and went just to please my mother. While sitting across the desk from the dean of women at the University of Pennsylvania, I noticed a print on the wall behind her.

The illustration was of Santa Sophia in Istanbul, one of my favorite buildings, and an example of splendid Byzantine architecture. During a pause in her perfunctory questioning, I asked the dean about the significance of the print and mentioned how much I loved that building and that time period. She was very impressed that I recognized it. She stopped talking to me in a formal interview format, and instead we had a very nice, very easy chat about Byzantine architecture and the archaeological museum at the University of Pennsylvania. From my passion for history of art and architecture, I knew a lot about Santa Sophia and archaeological museums. She was from Istanbul, Turkey! That is why she had the print on her wall. To my surprise, she accepted me on the spot, one of only seven transfer resident students.

What if I had never looked up and noticed the print behind her desk?

What if I had never asked the dean about it?

I would never have been accepted to the University of Pennsylvania.

Opportunity and Coincidence:
First Appearances Can Be Deceiving

Chatting and Curiosity

After completing graduate school in architecture, I traveled across the country to San Francisco. A cousin, an accomplished artist, told me that I absolutely had to meet a woman, a photographer in her eighties, named Imogen Cunningham. Several months passed, and I had forgotten my cousin's comment. I was volunteering at the first San Francisco International Film Festival. Assigned to the PR team, I was to meet and greet the directors and producers who came to the festival. Even better, I could see the films for free.

On opening day I went to the big theater and purposely sat one seat in from the aisle. There were many good-looking guys in the audience, and I hoped one would sit next to me in the empty seat. Instead, a little old lady with gray hair, somewhat hunched over and wearing a longish skirt and a beanie on her head, sat down in my open seat. *Just my luck*, I thought. *All these good-looking guys, and this little old lady sits in the seat next to me.*

Soon, all these guys my age started to come over to talk to her and hang around her. *Hmm, that is interesting. Who can she be?* I thought.

After a while everyone took their seats, and she turned to me and asked, "Are you a student, dear?"

Having just finished four years of college, and four years of graduate school, I was very, very pleased not to be a student anymore, and I boastfully said, "Oh no, I am definitely not a student anymore!"

"Oh, my dear, what a shame," she replied softly. "I hope to be a student all my life."

I felt like a shallow idiot.

By coincidence, she was Imogen Cunningham—the very same Imogen Cunningham I had hoped to meet. Not only was I sitting next to the very famous, outstanding photographer, but she was also the star of the delightful movie *Bed*, which we were about to see. No wonder everyone was gathering around her.

During intermission we talked and talked, and we shared each other's lunch. She was a close friend of photographer Ansel Adams. We agreed to meet every day for the next five days. We shared lunches and conversation and saw the films together. It also turned out that we lived across the street from each other. She would invite me to brunch on the weekends, when she would have other young people over. During these lunches she would reach under her day bed in the living room of her very small bungalow and pull out box after box of her incredible photographs. One in particular I remember was a well-known portrait of Cary Grant. A few days later she was injured and robbed in her darkroom. She was feisty and survived, and she continued to photograph until she died years later.

When my first child was born, my then-husband, John, and I celebrated by buying some fine arts photographs. The first purchase we made, in 1975, was one of her photographs and one of Ansel Adams's. Each time I look at her beautiful photograph of a magnolia blossom, I think of her comment: "I hope to be a student all my life."

That chance meeting was the beginning of my serious interest in collecting photography. Because of that interest, my oldest son, Wyatt Gallery, became a professional photographer. He says he was influenced by the photos that surrounded him growing up.

He and I are indebted to Imogen Cunningham and that chance encounter.

Opportunity and Coincidence: When My Father Met My Professor

Courage and Commitment

This story firmly illustrates the importance of perseverance, of having someone believe in you, and of believing in yourself. The surprise or chance meeting in the second part of the story must be an example of *luck*, synchronicity, or fate! It surpasses coincidence. It is the exception that proves my argument about luck.

Growing up, I was so directed. I had a plan. I had wanted to be an architect since sixth grade, and from that time I never lost sight of this intention. Later, as a seventeen-year-old high school student, I applied only to schools of architecture. Architecture programs then had a strict limit on female students. Only 10 percent of an incoming class could be female. This was at a time when women were not architects, and few were even admitted to schools of architecture. This was a time when admissions officers would say, "Women would take the place of a man who would support his family, and women would just get married and have babies and stay at home." This was before affirmative action laws, which became effective in the seventies.

Since most programs were small, about twenty or twenty-five students, that meant 2.5 women in the freshman class. I was one of only two women in my class, and one of four in the entire five-year architecture program.

Imagine my disappointment and discouragement when, returning home to Reading, Pennsylvania, at the end of my freshman year,

I learned that my grades in my architecture classes were all Ds and Cs.

Reading my report, my father declared sternly, "We are going to fly out to Cleveland to meet with your teacher." I was horrified. Then my father explained that he merely wanted to understand why I had received these grades.

Can you imagine being eighteen and having your father take you to meet with your professor? I dared not ask what my father would say, or what the tenor of the meeting would be. Dad was well known for both his charm and his temper.

In the professor's office Dad explained he was not asking to have the grades changed or to challenge the grades; he just wanted to understand how my work merited a D. Could he see some of my work?

The professor brought out my projects. Dad then asked if he could see some of the other students' projects. The professor displayed a classmate's project. Dad asked what grade it had received. The professor said, "An A."

"This is very beautiful. Clearly far superior to Leslie's. The drawings are meticulous," admitted my father.

Then my dad asked the professor if he could see some C-quality projects. Looking very annoyed, the professor disappeared for a few minutes and then returned with a couple other projects, which he displayed on a drawing table. Dad looked at them and then looked at mine. He asked the professor to explain the significant difference between my project, which received a D, and the projects that had received Cs.

"For one thing," the professor said, "she seems unable to produce decent architectural lettering." Then he hemmed and hawed and stuttered as he searched for other deficiencies.

Finally, in frustration, the professor exclaimed, "Well, there really is no significant difference. It is just that someone has to sort the good from the bad, those who will make it from those who will not! And clearly she will not make it in the field of architecture."

My father, quite calmly for him, especially given the situation, firmly told my professor, "Who are you to forecast the future of an eighteen-year-old—to say who will make it and who will not? Let me tell you something. If my daughter wants to become an architect, she will. And neither you nor I, nor anyone else will stop her from making it."

Then Dad turned to me, took my arm, and said, "There is no need for further discussion here. We're leaving." And we left. I changed my major from architecture to history of art, and I did very well. I also transferred to the University of Pennsylvania in my junior year.

But this is only half the story. The best is yet to come.

Four years later I was a graduate student in architecture and landscape architecture at the University of Pennsylvania, Graduate School of Fine Arts in Philadelphia. (one of three women in my class of thirty)

I was having a coffee in the lounge, in view of the main entry to the school, which overlooked the gallery in which the commended (A-quality) projects were displayed. Much to my disbelief, I saw my former architecture professor from Case Western Reserve walking through the entry, followed by about a dozen students.

I ran down the steps and tapped him on the shoulder, saying, "Hello, hello.

Do you remember me?"

Obviously surprised, he said with disdain, "Yes. I do."

I asked, "What are you doing here?"

He explained, "Well, this is the best school of architecture in the country, and I've brought some of my students here to visit Penn and see the students' projects."

And then, rather as an afterthought, he said with even greater disdain, "What are *you* doing here?"

I said, "I'm a graduate student here in the School of Architecture. In fact, the gallery is displaying the commended projects from the entire school. Mine was selected. Would you like to see it?"

Silence, then a grunt.

I walked him over to my project, an elementary school complex. He looked at it very, very carefully, still without a word. Then he bent over with his hands folded behind his back, to get an even closer look, and continued to examine my drawings in silence.

Finally, he straightened up, looked at me, and without emotion said, "Well, you still can't letter like an architect."

And then he turned and walked away, without another word.

These exchanges taught me that teachers or experts are not always right and that I must listen to myself and rely on my determination. Many times in the future, I would consider my view versus that of the "expert," and many times I proved them wrong. I had grown and matured, while my former professor was still trapped by the same limited thinking.

In retrospect it is clear just how much a parent's attitude toward you can encourage you or shut you down. My father always told me that I could do anything I wanted; he had no sympathy for giving up. Giving up was not an option.

Thankfully, I had not let this professor's narrow attitude discourage me or squelch my enthusiasm for architecture. And, thankfully, I did not give up. In the beginning of graduate school, the program was so difficult for me, many evenings I went home to cry from frustration or exhaustion. One boy said to me, "This program is going to take you four years of graduate school. Are you seriously going to spend four years here?" I replied that time goes by anyhow, and I would rather spend the time here becoming an architect!

I did not quit, and I did not give up, and eventually I got the hang of it and excelled. And I loved every minute of school from then on.

Willpower and perseverance.

Willpower, perseverance, and *hard work*!

I cannot say that enough!

I may not have gone where I intended to go, but I think I have ended up where I need to be.

—Douglas Adams, *The Long Dark Tea-Time of the Soul*

Conclusion

In the course of what appears to be zigzagging, my commitment and goal has always been the same: an advocate for good design with a passion for information design, architecture and cities. Rather than take the expressway or the turnpike—the most direct route, the straight line—I have taken the detours and side roads. Being open to these detours has made for a rich and varied life. As an architect, I have not made the traditional choices. By coming from another direction, as an architect, I have influenced the design and quality of our surroundings. I have certainly seen that the most direct route is not necessarily the best route to get you to where you want to go—or where you can be most effective. Within the broad field of architecture and design, the zigzags have taken me to places I had not originally imagined.

I hope these stories will be helpful to you in integrating your family life and business life with more satisfaction, and in reducing your inevitable anxieties. With planning and design, you can increase the opportunity to live where you want and work the schedules that you want, with the people with whom you want to be each day, and on projects that are invigorating and useful!

You can have it all; you just have to rethink "all"!

Once again, I am now in transition. It is again uncomfortable. I am looking for my next passion—my next total commitment. For me, transitions, *the times in between*, are always a challenging time.

Imogen Cunningham's comment continues to inspire me: "Oh, my dear ... I hope to be a student all my life."

And I will.

About the Author

Leslie is most frequently asked, "How do you balance your career with your family and raising your children?" Her response is: "I do not. I *integrate* my family and my career."

Leslie is an architect and a landscape architect who has never built a single building (except her own house.) Instead, she built successful businesses and organizations, while raising two children. Using the elements of design, Leslie goes beyond just planning and beyond goal-setting to teach you the steps to create the life you have always dreamed of. Nothing woo-woo here. Solid ideas full of wisdom, research, and humor.

Elected to the American Institute of Architects College of Fellows, Leslie has served on the board of the American Architectural Foundation and as an overseer of Penn Design University of Pennsylvania. The recipient of three design fellowships from the National Endowment for the Arts (NEA), she was selected as the USA Fellow by the NEA.

As CEO of the Society for Environmental Graphic Design (SEGD), Leslie rebuilt the organization into a substantial international membership and education resource.

Prior to SEGD, Leslie founded Philadelphia's Foundation for Architecture, a civic platform for urban planning and public participation. She has produced lectures, tours, design competitions, and guidebooks, as well as Philadelphia's award-winning direction and attraction sign program.

Since retiring from SEGD, Leslie has been a student of digital signage technologies, and immersive environments which are transforming art, architecture, exhibits, retail, and theater. She has lectured and written articles on this expanding field and produced internationally attended workshops.

Her favorite places to visit are the kingdom of Bhutan, in the Himalayas, and the American Southwest. Most of her adult life was spent in Philadelphia, Pennsylvania, raising her two sons. Leslie resides with her husband, Dick Dilworth, in the small village of Galisteo, New Mexico, where the skies are an intense blue, the air clean and crisp, the views limitless, and the culture diverse.

Website   www.lesliegallery-dilworth.com
Email   lesliegd@me.com